SIZZLING SEX
IN 30 DAYS

ROZ VAN METER

A member of Penguin Group (USA) Inc.

ALPHA BOOKS

Published by the Penguin Group

Penguin Group (USA) Inc., 375 Hudson Street, New York, New York 10014, USA

Penguin Group (Canada), 90 Eglinton Avenue East, Suite 700, Toronto, Ontario M4P 2Y3, Canada (a division of Pearson Penguin Canada Inc.)

Penguin Books Ltd., 80 Strand, London WC2R 0RL, England

Penguin Ireland, 25 St. Stephen's Green, Dublin 2, Ireland (a division of Penguin Books Ltd.)

Penguin Group (Australia), 250 Camberwell Road, Camberwell, Victoria 3124, Australia (a division of Pearson Australia Group Pty. Ltd.)

Penguin Books India Pvt. Ltd., 11 Community Centre, Panchsheel Park, New Delhi—110 017, India

Penguin Group (NZ), 67 Apollo Drive, Rosedale, North Shore, Auckland 1311, New Zealand (a division of Pearson New Zealand Ltd.)

Penguin Books (South Africa) (Pty.) Ltd., 24 Sturdee Avenue, Rosebank, Johannesburg 2196, South Africa

Penguin Books Ltd., Registered Offices: 80 Strand, London WC2R 0RL, England

International Standard Book Number: 978-1-59257-850-4
Library of Congress Catalog Card Number: 2008931272

11 10 09   8 7 6 5 4 3 2 1

Interpretation of the printing code: The rightmost number of the first series of numbers is the year of the book's printing; the rightmost number of the second series of numbers is the number of the book's printing. For example, a printing code of 09-1 shows that the first printing occurred in 2009.

Printed in the United States of America

To Robert Goodman for all your laughter and tenderness, the two sexiest qualities I know. Thanks also for defining romance as ingenious loving attention. What a concept! and what fun to explore.

CONTENTS

APPENDIXES

CONTENTS

INTRODUCTION

My name is Roz Van Meter, and for 30 years I've been an AASECT Certified Sex Therapist and Licensed Marriage and Family Therapist, helping thousands of couples escape a boring, stuck, or dysfunctional sex life. Most of them have come to realize that sizzling sex is primarily a journey of pleasure, that the journey is more important than the destination. True, a climax can whiz you momentarily into outer space or set off fireworks behind your eyelids, but sensualists who learn to savor every step of the journey are the best love-makers in the world.

The ideal is different for everybody. For some, sizzling sex connotes hot, heaving, throw-down ravishment. For others, it's ecstatic flights of sensuality. Still others want sweet, slow-moving, soul-connection bliss that satisfies both partners. Many want every one of these modes at different times.

Because I can see only a certain number of clients personally, and given the reality that so many people don't have access to a Certified Sex Therapist, I decided to write this do-it-yourself sexual solutions book, offering education, tips, techniques, and encouragement to people I may never get a chance to meet. *Sizzling Sex in 30 Days* offers the same outcome-oriented experience you would get by investing in a series of sessions with me, or by seeing any other certified sex therapist.

If you are experiencing a dry spell (or a major drought) in your sexual relationship with a spouse or lover, I've designed this program to help the two of you reclaim all the wonderful sexy energy that marked the beginning of your romance. You deserve it! One of my core beliefs is that healthy sex is a lifelong birth right.

You were born with exuberant sensuality. You may not remember it, but before the world started toning it down, your sexiness was natural, open, innocent, and lots of fun. I know a 3-year-old boy whose mother is delighted when he strips off his pajamas, streaks out the back door toward the pool, and hollers, "It's naked boy!" as he cannonballs into the water. We all experienced this little boy's exuberance as infants and children.

The good news is, you don't need to give it up just because you're older or have more responsibilities in life. A healthy, vibrant sensuality can wake you up and make you feel more alive than you've been since you were a toddler. It can create a new level of intimacy in your relationship, perhaps deeper than you've ever known.

A lot of education and training went into this book: four years of college, two years of graduate school, a Master's degree in Communication in Human Relations, and 3,000 hours of clinical experience just to get licensed as a Professional Counselor and Marriage and Family Therapist. Even so, OJT (on-job training) has taught me the most: I've worked with some wonderful clients and watched them reclaim their connection and rekindle their passion. Sometimes I tell you some of their stories, with names and circumstances changed to protect their privacy and confidentiality. I send deep thanks to them all.

It's important for you to know that *Sizzling Sex in 30 Days* is a sex-coaching program, not psychotherapy. Coaching is for healthy people who want more of something—or less of something. Maybe they need better balance in their lives, more time and energy, better communication and understanding, a more satisfying sex life, better information, education, and skills.

If you need psychotherapy or marriage therapy, contact your local mental health association for names of qualified psychological professionals in your area. For sex therapy, go to the website of the American Association of Sex Educators, Counselors, and Therapists (www.AASECT.org) to see if there is a Certified Sex Therapist in your area. However, I suggest that you first apply the contents of this book. You may decide you don't need the referral after all.

To get the most of what I offer in the *Sizzling Sex* program, you must take charge of your emotional and sexual life. Ask yourself, what do you want less of and more of in your life? If you're like most people, you want less stress and more *life* in your life. *Less* frustration, inhibition, miscommunication, tension, pressure, missed cues, strain, distance, even loneliness. *More* fun, sexiness, spontaneity, closeness, reassurance, sensual pleasure, and connectedness with your loved one.

Every exercise or suggestion is designed to help you reconnect with yourself and each other. You'll take steps to move past embarrassment, unresolved hurts, anxieties, and disappointments in your sexuality. You will learn how to wake up and notice things you may never have recognized, thought of in quite that way, or considered important. You can learn to pay attention to what's going on in your body, with your emotions, and with your spirit, as well as those of your partner.

You already know some of the information in this book. However, if you leave a tool in a drawer or ignore an instruction book, you might as well not own them. They become valuable only when you remember where they are and then use them purposefully. Some of the information may be new to you. I believe this book contains the information you need to re-create (or perhaps create for the first time) the kind of passion and sensuality you want and were meant to have.

Time to get started! Get out your calendar and mark 30 days from the time you start using this book. If you follow these suggestions, strategies, and approaches, I believe you'll see a real difference in your sexual skills and enjoy a deeper intimacy with the one you love.

Chapter 1

EXPECTATIONS

It's time to get cozy, light an aromatic candle, and put on some relaxing music because you're about to utilize all your senses to rekindle your sexual expression and deepen your connection to the one you love. We begin with some ways to talk about the program with your partner so you both can share the excitement as you enter the *Sizzling Sex* pleasure zone.

MAKE IT PERSONAL FOR YOU AND YOUR PARTNER

Did you know that human beings are (almost) the only species on earth that has sexual intercourse just for pleasure? The only exception is the Bonobo ape of Central Africa, which has replaced aggression with sex and is said to "do it" pretty much all the time. All the other species with which we share this planet can have sex *only* when the female is fertile. It's a biological imperative, done wholly without choice to continue the species.

Although it's fun to act like animals sometimes, it's also wonderful to know that, as human beings, you have the gift of sex as a choice.

Sex can be shared not only to make babies, but also as the tender, passionate expression of love and appreciation.

That leads me to an essential premise for *Sizzling Sex in 30 Days*. You don't need to know or do anything in advance to get the most out of the *Sizzling Sex* program. Unlike school, there are no prerequisites other than a desire for fun and sexual fulfillment with your partner of choice.

The *Sizzling Sex* program is 30 days of sensual or sexual activities. Each is explained and offered for you and your partner to consider, discuss, perhaps try, or skip entirely in favor of another.

Here's your opportunity to try things you've always been curious about. For example, have you wondered how couples get started in sexual role-plays, but were too embarrassed to ask? What about oral sex? For many couples, it's a tricky subject, so they steer clear of it. On these and many other aspects of sexuality, I give you gentle guidance and a step-by-step plan for getting past the detours that may have limited your sex in the past.

I'll nudge but never push you. You always have the option of moving backward or forward in the program. You can also make up your own "extra credit" activities. This book is designed as a springboard to get you going and on your way to sexual happiness. But I cannot emphasize enough the importance of making this program your own by using it in a way that reflects yours and your partner's unique personal preferences. Case in point: if I asked what *you* think is sexy, there's only one thing I could guarantee about your answer. It would be different than mine, or the lady (or man) next door's.

One Size Does Not Fit All

The pervasive "one size fits all" approach to sexuality is my biggest pet peeve as a sex coach. To counter it, I offer "crazy myths" throughout this book. These are false beliefs, often vestiges of earlier times, telling us what we *should* feel or do sexually just because someone else does—as if we're all the same person.

- Different Expressions, Same Level of Pleasure -

Crazy myth: If you don't holler and thrash around in bed, and if the earth doesn't move for you, you're undersexed. This is not true. Just as some of the most loving people *show* their love more than talk about it, some of the sexiest people alive carry their sexual response deeply. Some people are deeply satisfied with the exciting and reaffirming closeness of sex and don't even need an orgasm to be fulfilled.

I'm not talking about *indifference*, but rather a difference in what it takes to feel sexually gratified. It might surprise you to know that a difference in style, pace, and dramatic intensity of arousal varies more from person to person than it does from gender to gender.

Obviously, there are gender differences in the rate and degree of all kinds of emotional and sexual responses, including anger and tenderness, but these are no greater than differences among men and women. The bottom line is, we all have our own style of responsiveness. Everybody is unique. This is a scientific fact.

How to Begin the Conversation

Right now, sizzling sex may be nothing more than a vague and distant memory to you. Never fear. Sex is like riding a bicycle—once learned, the skill stays with you always. So does the feeling of joy as you feel the wind on your face on the way down a hill you haven't traversed for a long, long time.

The image of a plume of light and heat rising from a match is another good one to keep in mind as we begin. One small spark can start a fire. But to fan the flames of sexual desire in your relationship, you must first relight the embers that may be lying dormant within you.

This is both a physical and a mental process. You'll notice that the program kicks off on Day 1 with *self-awakening exercises* to enlist all five of your senses in this process.

Presenting *Sizzling Sex*

Maybe you and your partner are on the same page. You are both committed to improving your sex life. That's great! On the other hand, you may be at a stand-off, with one partner desiring more sex. Presenting the idea of *Sizzling Sex in 30 Days* requires careful communication.

The most important thing at the beginning is to present the program positively. "Here's something that sounds fun for us" is a thousand times better as an invitation than "Because our sex life is so boring (or gone), maybe this will help." Don't make it sound like another chore on a "to-do" list. Give the prospect of your sexual reawakening a sense of celebration, a renewal.

One issue to consider is timing—when to bring the idea to your partner's attention. Clearly, some times are better than others. The other equally important issue is how you receive your partner's reaction to trying the program. If you sense a lack of enthusiasm, don't interpret it as a message about you. First consider these questions:

- Is he exhausted from trying to do too many things in too little time?
- Is she in mourning from a loss?
- Is she just getting over a physical problem or childbirth?
- Is he worried about a business deal or the possible loss of a job?

Throughout this program, different exercises address the challenge of how you can effectively communicate with your partner from different angles. And by "angles," I don't mean sexual positions. Communication is verbal, visual, and tactile.

One of my goals is to teach my clients, and you, to enlist the most sensitive and sensual part of the body in every part of their sexual relationship—*the mind.* You must align what you say with how you touch and how you hear your partner. If there's one word to characterize the way you need to be at the start of this program, it's **open.** By this, I mean not judgmental; you should not assume you already know everything about your partner's feelings and desires. Most of all, you must be willing to find out.

Because this program is not intended as marriage therapy, we approach communication in a more playful way than you would in a therapist's office. At the same time, there's no reason not to borrow from the therapist's toolbox, when appropriate.

SHARE WITHOUT BLAMING, SHAMING, OR INFLAMING

Here's a quickie lesson from *Marriage Therapy 101*.

If you want to tell your spouse something about his behavior that's bothering you, without making him defensive, learn the difference between an I-message and a you-message.

Let's say you feel he's being critical of you when he walks in the front door, looks at the disarray of toys and clothes in the living room, and says "Jeez, what a mess." In response, you may lash out at him, saying, "I work all day, too. You're always making it my fault!" Or you can say, "Hey, honey, when you talk to me like that, I get hurt or resentful, and then I can't listen to what you're saying."

On the other hand, you could choose not to take it personally. Just grin and say, "Isn't it? We had a wild and wooly time around here today!" What may have begun as his criticism can be defused into a simple (and obvious!) observation.

The you-message blames and inflames. The I-message speaks to the issue at hand and deescalates the argument. Always use I-messages when discussing difficult topics with your spouse.

Make an agreement that you both will choose not to be defensive. Remember, if your partner asked you to pass the salt, it wouldn't mean there's anything wrong with the steak; at that moment, she's simply in the mood for salt. She's sending a message about herself and her preferences, not about you.

So where are we now? I hope you and your sweetheart have decided to give *Sizzling Sex* a try. There's nothing (but boredom and frustration) to lose and everything (like joy and ecstasy) to gain.

Chapter 2

THE FACTS OF LIFE

Just as an artist becomes intimate with the ingredients in his paints and learns how they'll interact with his canvas, you must become a connoisseur of your body's capabilities for sexual pleasure with your partner. Even though you've lived for decades in your body, I'm betting there are things you still don't know about its capability for heightened sexual experience and even ecstasy. Read on to discover exactly what I mean.

BODY: THE ANATOMY OF SEXUAL PLEASURE

Some basic facts about male and female anatomy will help you enjoy your sexual passion to the fullest. Many of these are not taught in school, nor are they discussed in families. The result is an absence of knowledge—or, worse, a lot of *mis*information about our human bodies that can do more harm than having no information.

Let's start with a very basic anatomy lesson. It may surprise you to learn that, in the womb, all fetuses begin as females. If chromo-somes have predetermined that the baby will be male, at a certain point in its development the fetus is flooded with hormones (this is called the *androgen bath*) that turn its sexual organs into those of a male. What would have been ovaries if the baby were a female move down in the body and become testes. And the same organ that began its development as a clitoris becomes a penis. No wonder there is so much similarity between male and female sexual responses. Yet many people seem to think males and females come from different planets.

A lot of people also seem to think that their own genitals belong to a different species than the rest of their body. Where did such a weird idea come from? This is not a rhetorical question. It really is a good idea to look at where you formed your ideas and values for and against your body, sensual pleasure, and sexuality. When you do, you'll realize that many came from your family, neighborhood, part of the country, church or synagogue, or schoolyard. Perhaps you've never examined these ideas and values to decide whether they actually reflect your own life experience.

A few years ago at a workshop on sexuality, I asked the audience, "What are some of the messages, spoken and implied, that you got about sex?" Various people in the audience called out the following:

"Nice girls don't."

"A guy shouldn't take 'no' for an answer—it probably means 'yes.'"

"If a guy's a virgin, he's a wimp. If a girl's not a virgin, she's a slut."

Remember, these workshop participants were sharing the messages they'd received from their upbringings and backgrounds. One woman near the back said the message in her family was, "We won't talk about it."

Then a woman in the first row said, "We won't talk about what?"

The whole audience laughed, but they knew what she meant. Sex is the unspeakable subject in a lot of families. And that sad fact hasn't changed much in the last few decades, despite what many see as the saturation of sex in popular culture. The irony is, sex is omnipresent. It helps sell soap and perfume, but somehow we still don't talk about it or consider it a healthy, natural part of life.

I believe that this double message—sex is great, sex is bad—is the reason so many people think of their genitals as ugly or nasty. Or they feel embarrassed and shameful about their sexual desires. It's the confused message they got while growing up. Most communication is nonverbal. A wrinkled nose, a gently slapped hand, or a gasp of disapproval can all shape a small child's attitudes.

After all, grown-ups are *supposed* to know everything, so if they act like *down there* is nasty, the child thinks it must be. Well, it isn't. It's tender and sensitive and private, but there's nothing nasty about it. The people who communicated this message, parents or preachers, probably didn't mean to confuse us, but the confusion was passed on through their attitudes and behaviors.

Given all the negative programming, it's not surprising that so many people aren't familiar with their genitals. It's ironic, isn't it? Here is the location of some of the greatest pleasure a human being can experience—not to mention its primary purpose of carrying on the human race—yet these parts of our bodies remain uncharted territory for many adults.

The good news is, you're never too old to learn something new. Here are a few simple steps to help familiarize you with your sexual anatomy. Do them alone or with your partner.

Ladies, Get Acquainted with Your Body

Grab a mirror and head for the bed. Prop your back comfortably on a couple of pillows, and put your feet flat on the bed, knees bent. Now prop the mirror in such a way that you can see between your legs. You may also want to aim a flashlight at the mirror so that it bounces light back onto the target zone.

Notice how much your genitals (vulva) look like a flower or a sea anemone. No, really! The outer petals (lips, labia) are furry, like the fuzz on some petals, then the inner ones are pink and roselike, framing the heart of the flower, the opening to the vagina.

At the top of the inner petals is the clitoris, a little pea-size pink organ. At least, in a lot of women it's pea-size. In others, it barely peeks out at all. In some, it looks like a miniature penis.

It's news for many to learn that, in male fetuses, the clitoris becomes the penis. The clitoris has a shaft that is hidden back in the body, and the little button that shows is the head of the clitoris. Like the penis's head, it is filled with very sensitive nerve endings. Like the penis, it becomes erect when it fills with blood through arousal.

If you could see inside your vagina, you would see a rose-color purse made of what looks like glistening satin. It has folds like a collapsed balloon, which will smooth out when it is enlarged, the way a balloon does when it's blown up. (*Caution:* Don't ever let your partner blow into your vagina. It's dangerous to your fallopian tubes.)

A Woman Aroused

When a woman is aroused, first, her vagina gets wet. We used to think the lubrication came from glands inside the vagina, but research tell us that the lubrication comes through the walls of the vagina, the way moisture beads up on an iced tea glass on a warm and humid day.

Here's what else happens when a woman becomes sexually aroused:

- Blood pulses down into her pelvic region (throbbing feeling)
- Her genital area swells and gets darker, rosier
- Her clitoris swells and emerges from its hood
- Her vagina balloons, becoming larger and more flexible

You, as a woman, have a special and unique gift. Your clitoris exists solely to give you pleasure. It has no other function in the human body. God/nature designed you so that you would desire and enjoy sex.

WHAT GETS HER HOT?

Crazy myth: Sexy women are always hot to trot. So if you aren't (hot to trot whenever your partner is), you aren't a sexy woman.

This one does a lot of damage, so let's dispel it right now. In the early 1970s, sex research pioneers Masters and Johnson described the human sexual response as having these phases in this order: desire, arousal, plateau (getting close to climax), orgasm, and what they called the refractory period, basically the time it took for the man to get hard again. For 30 years, that was the model. However, it turns out that this sequence describes the *male* response cycle. Women might trip lightly up those steps in that order, but not always.

Many a woman doesn't start with desire. Desire pops into the picture after she has been kissed, fondled, kissed, stroked, caressed, and kissed again. (Yes, guys, many women find kissing to be a strong aphrodisiac). In other words, for women, arousal may actually precede desire. I'll tell you more about that later, but do bear it in mind.

Gentlemen, It's Your Turn

You know more about your penis and testicles than your lady knows about herself, for two reasons. First and most obvious, they're out there in plain sight. Second, boys often get more implied permission to talk about sex than girls do. However, you may have been brain-washed to buy into the *Cult of Competitiveness,* which is truly crazy where equipment is concerned.

SIZE ISN'T EVERYTHING

Another crazy myth: The bigger the penis, the better the action (more virile, more manly, more studly).

Well, it's not true. Simply not true. Any woman with an average-size vagina prefers skilled lovemaking to a baseball bat any day of the week. A few women whose anatomy is different have loose vaginas and like the feeling of being "filled up" with a large penis. However, the nerve endings that give the most pleasure are just a little way into the vagina, not at the back. If you are average-size or even a bit smallish when erect, you can be a wonderful lover and satisfy virtually any woman. What's equally important, you can satisfy yourself.

Now, back to a man's anatomy. Men, you will see a bridge of skin between your scrotum and anus. That bridge, called the perineum, covers a muscle that is part of the interconnected pelvic muscula-ture. Try contracting this muscle, as if you were trying to pick up a marble with your anus. Did your penis move? It will when it's erect. More about this magic muscle later.

A Man Aroused

When a man is first aroused, blood rushes to your pelvic area; you can feel the throb of your pulse in that area as blood begins to fill the chambers of your penis. There is a kind of hydraulic valve into each chamber that closes the door when the chamber is full, preventing the blood from draining back out until you have reached your climax or are distracted and lose the erection (which is temporary—more about that in Chapter 9).

This flooding of blood into the penis converts it from a soft penis to a hard cock, or whatever nickname you and your partner prefer. As you men have discovered, although you urinate out of the same opening as you ejaculate, you can't do both at once. A shunt inside you turns the urethra from a urine-tube to a semen-tube.

Okay, let's review what happens when a man gets sexually aroused:

- His blood pulses down into your pelvic region (throbbing feeling)
- His genital area swells and gets darker, rosier
- His penis swells and emerges from its hood, if he's not circumcised
- Moisture—like tears, only more slippery—appears as lubrication from his penis

Now, ladies and gentlemen, does this sequence of arousal sound familiar? Exactly. That's because male and female sexual responses are a great deal alike physically. What's different, obviously, is that a woman's vagina is constructed to *receive* and a man's penis is built to *enter.* His enlargement changes his penis from a soft, tender organ (Lady Chatterley thought of her lover's sleeping penis as a rose) to a rigid organ, as if it were a hard muscle covered with satiny skin and a foam-rubber tip for your comfort. A man's enlargement occurs so he can comfortably accommodate entry into the female body. Both of you have lubrication for ease of entering and highly aroused nerve endings for pleasure.

Perhaps now you feel more comfortable exploring each other's genital area. Some of my clients get a kick out of naming each other's genitals. They enjoy the playfulness of saying something like, "Earl sure is up and looking around this morning." If that's not your style, don't do it. But if it is, it can add a teasing, playful note that reduces anxiety about discussing sex.

The Hygiene Factor

Many parts of your body that are closed off from air, including feet, armpits, and genitals, regularly get sweaty and need to be bathed. However, if they haven't gone too long without a bath, their smells are good, healthy, musky smells. Think of the difference between someone who has just come back from a three-mile run and his smells of salty, fresh sweat, and the street person who hasn't bathed in days or weeks. *Big* difference.

It's ironic that advertisers have brainwashed us to believe that healthy, fresh body odor is gross. Of course, they sell their "hygiene" products by manipulating our insecurities. The irony is doubled when you consider that traditionally we used the musk of other animals, designed to send sexual messages, as the base ingredient of perfumes to cover our own. Amazing. Still, some people are crazy about their partner's natural smell: good, clean sweat, the bakery smell of some genitals. Others aren't. Perhaps they have old "nasty" mental programs running about sex, or their partner's scent is less subtle than some.

But these are the facts: if kept clean (wiped properly, bathed regularly), the genital area probably contains fewer germs than your mouth. And speaking of mouths, I guess you know that great lovers through the centuries have spoken of a woman's vulva as "the other mouth" and loved soul-kissing it.

MIND: GIVE YOURSELF PERMISSION FOR PLEASURE

Very often, as any relationship grows from its early blissful days to midlife or maturity, let's say after the first six or seven years, "real life" tends to get in the way of a sizzling sex life. As a couple, you may think nostalgically about the infatuation of your early romance and the passionate, frequent sex that made it so much fun, but you may also have devalued regular sex as less worthy of your time and energy now that you've taken on the responsibilities of managing a household, making a living, and nurturing a family.

Make *Sizzling Sex* a Priority

Of course, it's important to grow up and be responsible, but you don't have to throw out the baby with the bath water! Without fully realizing it, by putting it way below the other *important* things in your lives, you may be snuffing out the sexual desire that initially kindled your attraction to each other, and putting your relationship at risk.

When you consider yourself so noble (and you are) for working overtime to score a promotion and still show up at every one of your child's soccer games—or when you wake up early on Sunday to improve your golf swing or master a new recipe but can't remember when you last had fabulous, sizzling sex with your partner—it's time to reexamine your priorities.

We forget that only within a long-term, committed relationship do we get to play out the natural ebb and flow of sexual desire and, in the process, learn how to keep this vital life force and the relationship going strong. And if that sounds too "pie in the sky" to worry about when you've got a kid to pick up from school and a memo to write for your boss before you can leave the office, remember this. The old saying holds true here as elsewhere: *use it or lose it.*

While I'm on this subject, here's another good one. *All work and no play make Jack (or Jill) a dull boy (or girl).* If you let your sex life go, you're missing out on the fun you deserve as a full-blooded man or woman in the prime of your life!

And as far as I'm concerned, wherever you are is the prime of your life!

In the next chapter, I give you a primer on the basic working parts of my program. From there, get ready to sizzle!

Chapter 3

Your Recipe for Sizzling Sex

The best palate-tested recipes give you a complete list of ingredients and the basic steps to follow, but they can also allow for last-minute spontaneity, time for flavors to blend, and slight variations every time you make the dish. Most important, the cook feels no pressure to hurry. And your sex life, like a scrumptious meal, should not be fast food!

How to Approach the Program

If you're someone who works better step-by-step, my *Sizzling Sex* program is a perfect recipe for you exactly as it is. Each of the next five chapters contains six days of activities designed to help you and your partner relax, reconnect through talk and touch, add romance to your lives, and find new ways to play—all intended to turn up the temperature of your sexual relationship. If you follow the program as written, I predict that by Day 30, you'll be ready for a uniquely pleasurable graduation ceremony: a sizzling dream date where you can apply everything you've learned.

What If We Can't Complete the Program in a Month?

Relax. Just because I've arranged 30 days of activities in a particular sequence doesn't mean you need to follow the program in this order, or even daily. Whatever you do, don't put *Sizzling Sex* on your household to-do list. Whether because of scheduling demands or just personal preference, you may choose to move at a more leisurely pace.

Another approach is to cut these ideas into little strips, fold them, put them in a bowl, and draw one out at random. If you aren't in the mood for that one, put it back and draw another. You can rig the lottery to your own satisfaction.

How Soon Should We "Do It?"

How soon you and your partner get to the Main Event is entirely up to the two of you, but I recommend that you hold off until Day 12.

Perhaps your sexual charge will build till there's smoke coming out your ears. Or maybe you haven't been sexual with each other for a long time, in which case another week-and-a-half wait is fine. In any case, you won't die from lack of sex and meantime you'll be in training for closer, more wonderful sex from now on.

GETTING COMFORTABLE

By waiting to consummate your sizzling sex, you can prepare yourself, body and mind, to make the most of it. But what if your mind says you should be ashamed of your body, or you mustn't have any fun, play, or relaxation until you've attended to all your duties? Then perhaps you are two quarts low on fun, play, and relaxation, and

embarrassed about the current state of your figure or physique—
which isn't the same as your body. I hope *Sizzling Sex* will help you
learn the difference.

Our attitudes and values are shaped by our history—not only what
we experience firsthand, but what we are told and what we see
on television, read in books, see in magazine ads or on billboards,
and observe in other people's interactions. If all we see 24/7 is the
fashion model's "perfect" skinny body and flawless complexion, and
the news announcer's 1,000-watt smile, we may come to believe
we can't possibly measure up as we are. How sexual does that make
you feel? Not very.

The net effect of so many messages saying "You're not good
enough" can take a hefty toll on your self-image. You may be so
accustomed to this channel of negativity that you're not even aware
you've integrated it into your self-concept.

Remember, by looking at all this, you are not blaming anyone, including yourself. You are simply noticing what your programming and
experience have been. From the time you were born, you have been
writing programs for yourself based on your perception of reality.
These programs create messages you send yourself, consciously
or subconsciously, about your appearance, intelligence, self-worth,
ability to love and be loved, and so on. The resulting self-talk then
has a powerful impact on your bodily response. If you're sending
put-down messages, they can actually tamp down your sexual desire
and response.

Then there are all of society's double, often contradictory, messages
about sex in general. It's bad. It's good. It's a natural part of life, but
you shouldn't like it too much. Only "bad" girls really *like* sex. Men
are incapable of really *loving* the same woman they have hot sex
with. Is it any wonder people are confused about what they want
versus what they *should* want in a sexual relationship?

Once you understand the perceptual engines that are chugging away beneath the surface, you can re-engineer the ones that are outdated or just plain incorrect. You can keep what works for you and cheerfully discard what doesn't. You have already changed a lot of your attitudes and beliefs over the years—noticing, thinking for yourself, redeciding, maturing. Now you can do it systematically and on purpose, noticing and editing the self-defeating messages about body image and sex.

KEYS TO THE KINGDOM

I invite you to use this *Sizzling Sex* program as the first leg of a life-long journey. It's a journey back to you—you as the kingdom and you as an alive, sexual being free to love your partner with your body, heart, and soul. This kingdom I speak of is a place as magical as it is real. It's inside you, but as you open up to who you really are, you'll find you have more than enough of you to share with your beloved, and your beloved with you.

You need five keys, or essential elements, to make this journey. Think of them as the five necessary ingredients for your favorite recipe. These five keys are self-preparation, honest communication, sensual touch, romance, and fantasy.

Preparing Yourself

This is where you start to untangle the negative self-talk from the part of you that still longs for intimacy and a sizzling sex life with the one you love. You'll do this by answering a series of questions that delve into your attitudes and feelings about yourself, beginning with your early childhood up to the present day. I suggest that you set aside one or more sessions to do this, in 30- to 45-minute time blocks. This should be private time to reflect and write down your thoughts and feelings. Just let the responses flow from your fingers to the pen, without editing.

It's best to get a fresh new pad or notebook for this purpose, and dedicate it as your *Sizzling Sex Journal* for the duration of the program. Most of the men and women I've coached and counseled have reported that journaling is extremely helpful. Use your journal as an ongoing conversation with yourself, a place to record your ideas, triumphs, disappointments, realizations, and breakthroughs.

As you write down your answers, leave room for some questions and answers you might want to add for yourself, perhaps having to do with relationships, the roles of men and women, husband and wife, pleasure and play, and sexuality. After you've written all you can think of, come back later and start writing again. What you're seeking to uncover are answers to these questions.

- What were some of the early messages I got about men and women from my family, community, school, church, authority figures, and same-age friends—not only what they said, but what they implied?

- What effect have those messages had on my adult life? On my attitudes toward myself, my values about what's important, my body, and my personhood?

- How have I changed for the better over the years, and how do I want to continue changing?

My only advice as you complete this exercise: tell the truth and be kind to yourself.

Read over each of the following statements and write down a conclusion to each that's *true for you*.

- One of the messages, direct or implied, that I got from my father about sensuality/sexuality was …

- What he was trying to do for me was …
- One way this affects me today is …
- A way I could modify that to better fit for my life is …
- One of the messages, direct or implied, that I got from my mother about sensuality/sexuality was …
- What she was trying to do for me was …
- One way this affects me today is …
- A way I could modify that to better fit for my life is …
- As a child, I remember my father being joyful when …
- How that affects me today is …
- As a child, I remember my mother being joyful when …
- How that affects me today is …
- What comes to mind when I think of the word *passion* is …
- One of my father's favorite sayings was …
- How it affected me was …
- How I've changed his negative message to a positive is …
- One of my mother's favorite sayings was …
- How it affected me was …
- How I've changed her negative message to a positive is …

You and Your Body

By completing the next statements you will compare positive and negative feelings you have had in the past about your body. By reflecting on any negative self talk you've engaged in, I hope you will connect early attitudes you've uncovered with current, not so nice feelings you have about your body and sexuality. You may run into some uncomfortable feelings. If you do, please remember: by letting go of old attitudes that no longer serve you, you'll be able to clear a space for something new and exciting to replace them.

- What I like about my body is …
- How I am uncomfortable with my body is …
- The first time I felt pretty/handsome was …
- I felt sexy with my partner when …

Good work! Now let's move to how you feel and operate in relationship.

You in Relationships

You and your partner may wish to share your answers to these questions with each other, or you may prefer to keep them private, at least for now. An important objective of this program is to learn new ways to communicate on such sensitive matters. As you move through the days and weeks ahead, I predict that sharing with your partner will get progressively easier.

- I can be tender and express this to my partner. An example is …
- I can be critical and judgmental of my partner. An example is …
- I am becoming less judgmental. An example of this is …
- Loving others begins with loving myself. Three things I love about myself are …
- When I think of "happiness," I think of …
- When I think of "love," I think of …
- In my mind, I can say to someone, "I cannot make you happy, but I can …"

◊ A person I would like to say it to is …

◊ When I treat loved ones with respect, we all benefit. A recent example of that is …

Congratulations! You've completed the hardest part of the self-preparation process. Think of it as a spring cleaning of your sexual identity. Now get ready to fill the cleaned out spaces with some really good new ideas and attitudes.

Sharing

The second key to *Sizzling Sex* is the ability to communicate clearly with your partner. Good communication can heal misunderstandings, send love, and mend a hurting relationship. We all come with similar baggage in this area. Here are some of the common questions I get and answers I usually give.

Q: Why is it so hard for us to talk about things?

A: Maybe because we never learned effective communication at home.

Q: Why didn't our parents teach us?

A: Because no one taught them.

Q: What if when I talk about what I want or don't like or want more of, my partner doesn't hear it?

A: Sometimes he or she doesn't want to hear it, but usually it depends on how and under what circumstances you send the message.

Q: It's scary to put myself out there like that.

A: Of course it is, but it's a risk worth taking. Otherwise, how will you each know who the other is?

Okay, you may think, *but how should I be communicating?*

Try a little experiment. Go up to a mirror, look yourself in the eye, and say the following while jabbing your index finger accusingly at your image:

"Look at you! You look horrible! You need to get some rest!"

Notice what tone your voice takes. Talk about giving yourself the finger!

Now do it again, only this time, point the finger back at yourself, and say, "I'm looking and feeling tired. I need to get to bed earlier tonight."

Notice how much kinder your voice is. You're no longer blaming, just prescribing.

The same change occurs when you're talking to someone else and choose to send an I-message ("Honey, I need …") instead of a you-message ("You never …"), which can come across as criticism or even attack.

If you keep in mind that people are talking about themselves and their preferences, not about you, you can get past defensiveness, which is a sure-fire intimacy killer. The same principle applies in the bedroom as it does in the boardroom. Just ask directly and courteously for what you, and when someone asks you for what he or she wants, hear it as just that, a statement about what is wanted. Simple, isn't it? But so often overlooked. Instead, people get offended because the other person doesn't read minds.

It's the ultimate gotcha: "What's the matter, honey?" "Nothing." "Sure there is. I can tell. What's going on?" "Well, if you loved me, you'd know!" What a no-win situation for everyone.

─────── ## How to Ask for What You Want ───────

Here is my practically foolproof formula for communicating using an I-message. The next time you want to make a request (not a demand, not a criticism) of your partner, try using this template.

Let me tell you what's going on with me.

I'm feeling_____ about _____.

And what I'd like is _____.

───────────────────────────── ❧✿❧ ─────────────────────────────

Here's an example of a spouse asking effectively for she wants:

"Honey, I'm feeling lonesome for you. I've/you've been so busy with the (kids, project, job, whatever), and what I'd really like is for us to turn off TV and go make love."

That sure beats, "Do you realize how long it's been since you made love to me? What's the matter with you, anyway?"

Let's take that same principle into bed.

You-message: "Don't be so rough! Are you *trying* to hurt me?"

The effect: Negative.

Here's the I-message: "Oooh, baby, ease up a little. I'd like that a little softer. Oh, tha-a-a-t's it! That drives me wild."

The effect: Yummy.

Your body posture is also important for good communication. When you're the receiver, lean forward, pay attention, and really listen. Listen *into* what your partner is saying. Listen for the feelings. Listen with your heart as well as your ears. Listen as a friend, with kindness. Repeat back what your partner said, to be sure you understand it.

Here are some examples of repeating back a partner's statement until you're sure of his meaning:

Statement: "Why didn't you let me know you were going to be late? I've been up for hours, listening for your car."

Restatement: "So you're mad just because I got back late from the trip."

Statement: "No, that's not what I said. It's because you didn't call and *tell* me you were going to be late."

Restatement: "Okay, so it's not that I ran late, just that I didn't let you know."

Statement: "Right! Honey, next time give me a call. I was worried about the icy roads, and I wasn't sure what time you left."

Re-statement: "Okay, babe. Next time I'll call and give you a heads-up."

In summary, you both must ...

- Take turns being the speaker and the listener.
- Really listen and understand when that's your job.
- Keep your connection tight.
- Ask directly for what you want.
- Send I-messages, not you-messages.
- Request, don't criticize or blame.
- Be creative in finding ways to send your message.
- Carefully pick the time, place, and tone.

... you will be amazed by the results. I guarantee it.

The Miracle of Touch

The third key to the kingdom of *Sizzling Sex* is the art of touching and being touched. Being touched is a physiological mandate. Dog breeders and ranchers know that if a mother animal somehow abandons a newborn, the breeder must rub the baby with a rough cloth or it will die. This is a substitute for the friction of its mother's licking and nuzzling, to start its bodily functions.

Human beings need stroking, too. When wars create orphaned babies, sometimes there are more of them than their caretakers can adequately nurture. The babies get fed and changed but not cuddled and hugged, and they can waste away and die from severe absence of nurturing. We all need touching, and sometimes it needs to be a nondemand, no-expectations kind, whether it's a welcome home hug or the beginning of a sexual encounter.

Stroking is a crucial part of courtship. If you are in a romantic relationship now, think back to its beginning and all the loving attention you developed. Would you like to regain what was there? Or perhaps your personal sexuality had not yet matured before you got together. Perhaps you had limited experience, or maybe you received some strong (though perhaps subtle) antisexual messages when you were growing up. Maybe you had a demeaning sexual experience in your past. Think back, and see if you can get in touch with the way you were back then. Making this assessment will help you appreciate the development of sexuality in your relationship and allow you to focus on what you want more of right now.

Sensual focus is a beautiful way to re-romanticize yourself and your partner. During each week of the *Sizzling Sex* program, there is an activity designed for you and your partner to indulge in loving touch in a new place, time, or manner. Whether you're sharing a bath, giving a massage, or touching thighs and forearms while sitting in the movies, a mind/body focus on the sensual reminds you of this precious aspect of your loving relationship.

Isn't this obvious? Yes, it is. Then why are you so out of practice? Once again, familiarity and routine are the culprits. By practicing how to give and receive touch, you will slowly allow yourselves to become reacquainted sensually and sexually. In the days ahead, you'll revisit your first kiss, the time you first held hands. With a brand new awareness, you'll explore your bodies as if for the first time. In the process, you'll recover what may have been lost to time and habit.

Romance

Of all the women I've counseled over the years, I'd say that 95 percent want more romance. They want to receive affection in the morning and afternoon, not just at night as their clothes are coming off. They want to be treated as someone special, not all the time (that wouldn't be special, not to mention possible), but often.

Here's what may surprise you. About 80 percent of the men I've talked to say they want the same thing. So because romance appeals to women *and* men, you can work together to create an environment conducive to romantic expression and find new ways to deliver messages of romance to your beloved.

During your month of *Sizzling Sex* exercises, I offer suggestions on ways to reromance your partner and, in the process, re-enchant your relationship.

Fantasies

This last key to the kingdom is one of those areas you may have always wondered about but never got around to trying.

It is generally accepted that men have a lot of sexual fantasies. What is less well known is that women do, too.

In the 1990s, Nancy Friday wrote a book called *My Secret Garden.* It was based on a classified ad she put in major cities' newspapers, saying she was a serious researcher who was writing a book about women's sexual fantasies. Women willing to share theirs could either send an anonymous letter to a post office box or call a dedicated phone line and speak their fantasies, which were then recorded. (This was before caller ID. There was anonymity on both sides.)

Well! Dr. Friday's post office box filled up so quickly that it had to be periodically replaced with ever bigger ones, and the answering machine cassette had to be changed every few hours. Women were thrilled to finally be able to tell their innermost, highly charged sexual fantasies. Many of the ones Dr. Friday included are a bit bizarre, but they are safe because they are either make-believe or, in some cases, highly embellished memories. For those who wish to learn more, Dr. Friday's book is listed in Appendix B.

On Day 20, you'll learn how fantasy works to enhance sex.

Psychologists tell us that fairy tales, with all their scariness, are ways children can live out their aggressions vicariously and have it all come out all right. Sexual fantasies are similar. By imagining a titillating scene, we have a safety valve for that deep part of us that wants to do naughty things, or even aggressive or dangerous ones.

Millions of people read or watch hard- or soft-core porn, or think extravagantly sexy thoughts to get aroused. As long as it doesn't lead to behavior that disrespects, demeans, or endangers yourself or your partner, fantasize away!

Ready, Set, Go!

Now that you've completed your primer on the five keys to the kingdom, you're on your way to *Sizzling Sex.* Remember, you can always come back to tweak your relationship skills or re-examine your attitudes or self-talk whenever you want. It's a lifelong journey, but there's no better time than now to get started. I have no doubt that you're ready for Day 1.

Chapter 4

REIGNITE THE SPARK IN YOUR RELATIONSHIP

Many of us are busy chasing a career, kids, housework, and the calendar. We're going so fast that life can feel like chasing a runaway train. Have you noticed that no matter how fast you go, the train just keeps accelerating? You know what I mean. The days, weeks, and months seem to pick up speed. You take down the Christmas lights and wreath and, before you know it, it's time to get them back out and hang them again. Meanwhile, that wonderful, sexy, sensual excitement you used to feel with your partner gets shoved to the caboose of your runaway train.

Take heart, you are now beginning the journey back to a rich sexual connection with your beloved. With 30 simple activities, each given a day, you'll rebuild that essential foundation of your union, the one that helps the two of you sustain your relationship as you race through the rest of your busy lives. Best of all, this simple program can easily fit with and around those everyday responsibilities.

DAY 1: AWAKEN YOUR SENSES

Just as you cannot love someone else unless and until you love yourself, you cannot wholeheartedly respond to a partner's desire for sexual union without first feeling alive in your own body. Today's exercise shows you how to use all five senses to wake up your body and ignite your sexual passion.

It's pretty basic, isn't it? To enjoy your body, you must first be aware of it. The problem is, you may be using your body mostly as a vehicle to carry your head around, with its obsessive thoughts about to-do lists, appointments, calls to return, and e-mail to check.

You have to get out of your head and into your senses.

Here are some exercises to help you get grounded in your senses, in your body, and in the moment. Take your time in doing these exercises, and do them daily, especially as you begin the *Sizzling Sex* program. I suggest you take on each item one at a time. Read my instructions, then put the book down and complete the exercise before moving on to the next one.

Wake Up Your Eyes

Right now, look around you as if you were seeing the world for the first time. Notice the shapes of things: rectangles, circles and arcs, and amorphous shapes that are like nothing else.

Notice the pattern of light and shadow, and the colors around you, some subtle, some bright. Then notice the flicker of movement.

Experiment with seeing through squinty eyes as well. It gives a new shimmer to the world; sometimes you will not only see different things, but you will see things differently.

Did you know that more than 90 percent of the information you take in is through your gift of sight? Appreciate the gifts your eyes give you.

Wake Up Your Ears

Listen! What all can you hear? At first there are obvious sounds, but if you quiet your inner dialogue and really pay attention, there are other sounds—the hiss or roar of traffic, the hum of machinery, faint voices from another room, distant music. Get even quieter inside yourself, and you can hear your own breathing and heartbeat.

To hear your body more clearly, put plugs in your ears. Now the rhythm of your breathing is more audible. You can focus so completely on that rhythmic, surflike sound that it fills your whole awareness. Just think of all that breath, that column of life that your lungs create over and over until the final one. Amazing!

Wake Up Your Touch

Your skin is the largest organ of your body, and with it you literally feel your world. Those microscopic nerve endings all over the skin of your body are ready to convey warmth or chill, softness or sharpness, from the moment of your birth. That's how you first experience your world, through the sense of touch.

Move around and touch things. Find something furry; run your hand along something smooth. Curved. Prickly. Warm or cool.

Touch yourself. Really notice the textures of your body.

Answer these questions:

- How is the hair on your head different from that on your body?

◆   How are the soles of your feet different from the inside curve
where your arm bends at the elbow?

Then close your eyes and explore your little finger with the other
hand. It's like a fine Swiss watch, the way it is hinged, its tiny bones,
sinews, and muscles.

Now do the same with your thumb, and when you're finished, imagine how your life would be changed if you didn't have it.

Wake Up Your Senses of Taste and Smell

Sniff the air, your own skin, someone else's skin, a scented soap or
candle, a flower, a pungent food.

Cup your hands around an orange and feel its satin-dimpled surface.
Now slowly peel it, up close to your face, and feel it spray on your
cheek, and smell and taste its juice. Take a moment to appreciate
the absolute gorgeousness of an orange.

Take It Slow

Slowing down and finding your own rhythm can light up your sexuality. The best way to slow your mind and awaken your body is to pay
attention to your breathing. In our fast-moving, crazy world, it can
be hard to get into the slower pace required for deep breathing, but
here's an exercise to help you. Read over the sequence, then put the
book down and begin. If you do it with your partner, one can read
while the other relaxes, with eyes closed.

1.   S-l-o-w down. Pay attention. Don't be in a hurry about anything having to do with your sensuality. Be. Here. Now.

2.   Take energizing and relaxing breaths. Lie on your back and
get comfortable. Now put your hand on your belly, and take

a slow, deep breath. Pretend you are filling a pitcher with air. Feel your belly rise. Now exhale, letting your breath just float out.

3. Do it again. Take a deep, comfortable breath, and exhale it gently till your lungs are empty.

4. Do it a third time, only now imagine you are breathing in light and relaxation, and exhaling all of your anxiety and tension.

Any time you need to relax, repeat these sense-awakening exercises. They can be life changing.

Day 2: Unleash Your Imagination

How often do we just sit around and let our imaginations run wild? Not often enough. Today you're going to unlock your creativity and imagine you and your partner as the leading man and lady in a captivating new love story, one of your own making.

Start a *Sizzling Sex Journal*

Start today's exercise by selecting a fresh, new notebook to serve as your *Sizzling Sex Journal.*

Your objective in these journal exercises is to write down the first thoughts that come to mind in response to my questions—without censoring or editing yourself. In creative writing circles, it's called "free writing."

My first question for your journal: What was the last love story that moved you to tears?

Was it *Titanic* or *Atonement*? How about the book or movie of *Gone With the Wind*, or maybe *The Bridges of Madison County*? Who were your favorite male and female characters in these stories? What appealed to you about these leading men and women?

Have you made some notes? If not, do so now.

Now, with your journal and pen still within reach, close your eyes and take a moment to *become* these same characters.

Give the process at least a minute. What you're doing consciously here is what we do unconsciously every time we emotionally invest in a great love story. We identify with the characters. So become your favorite hero or heroine; give yourself permission to feel their longings for each other. Re-experience the most memorable moments, for example—the tension that hung in the air in the moments preceding their first kiss. Put yourself in that scene. Are you trembling with anticipation?

When you finish conjuring these scenes, open your eyes and jot down the first feelings, words, or images that come to you.

For your next journal exercise, we touch on something a bit more erotic. Try to remember the last thing you watched or read that *turned you on*.

Perhaps it was from a book of literary erotica, *Lady Chatterley's Lover* or *The Story of O*. Or, for the guys, did it come from an especially good issue of *Playboy*? Porn videos work for a lot of people by getting their imaginations and juices going. Allow these erotic images and encounters to enter your mind. When you can picture it clearly, open your eyes and write down in your journal what you saw.

─────── **A HINT FOR BEDTIME** ───────

Just before you fall asleep, give yourself permission to have enlightening, sexy dreams. Ask yourself, what does my desire feel like? Keep your *Sizzling Sex Journal* next to your bed to help you remember your dreams when you first wake up.

This last imagination exercise can be done on your way to a good night's sleep. After all, you're going to dream about *something*. Why not make it *wild*?

DAY 3: GETTING TO KNOW YOU ... AGAIN

Is your relationship like a well-worn shoe? You know what I mean. Is it comfortable and cozy but lacking the excitement you remember when it was fresh and new? Well, don't worry; there's still a treasure trove of things you and your partner don't know about each other simply because you haven't asked. This is the day when you start to uncover them and, in the process, find new intimacy in your relationship.

Sex is one vital form of intimacy for a couple. Honest, heartfelt communication is another. Often it takes one to get to the other. However, in one of those seemingly ever-present Mars and Venus dichotomies, women often prefer to talk before they have sex, while men can open up verbally only after intercourse. That's partly because, for men, actions speak louder than words.

And the opposite is true for most women.

What can be done to bridge this apparent gulf? You can find neutral ground in conversation. "How do you feel?" is not a good conversation starter. To a man, this question can be a real conversation stopper, not a starter. Instead, try one of the following structured communication exercises designed to give two partners a playful way to gain intimacy through honest, heartfelt communication—without any heavy agendas or unrealistic expectations.

Trading Places to Get Back to the Beginning

Remember when you and your beloved were still in the getting-to-know-you stage? You were each like a fascinating Christmas present waiting to be unwrapped. Now you know your partner better than in the beginning, but are you seeing him clearly or through the lenses of your own agendas? It's time to find out.

In this exercise, you trade places and give what you imagine might be your partner's answers to these questions.

- What do you think about the most or a lot?
- What is your greatest hope?
- What is your worst fear?
- What is your one true passion in life (other than your partner or children)?
- How have I contributed to who and how you are?
- When you were a child, what was delightful or scary?
- When you were growing up, how did your parents show their love for each other?

The point is to get closer, not to "get it right," so please speak with respect and fondness, putting your complaints on hold. When you feel the time is right, you might show your answers to your partner and ask whether either of you perceived the other correctly. The two of you can talk about how close you got to the other's perception.

Stay mindful to put yourself in your partner's place. A lot of us fall in the trap of sending affection the way *we* would like to receive it instead of sending on the other person's channel. If we don't pay attention to what channel a partner is on, our messages can whiz past our ears. There's no point in continuing to send on your own channel and being annoyed because your honey doesn't receive that way. Words and actions mean different things to each of us—another way of saying we're on different channels. To make sure you receive your partner's *intended meaning,* try repeating back to her what you've heard *using different words.*

Consider an example: speaking about a sexual position, she says, "I don't mind it." As her sexual partner, you might say, "But it sounds like it's not one of your favorite positions. Is that true? She then has your permission to expand on her feelings or preferences.

Here's a tip about talk for both men and women. If you begin to view your intimate talk times in the same way you do sex with your partner (as a time for intimate sharing) I guarantee you that both your sex and talk will improve exponentially.

Women tell me every day that they wish their partners would have intimate conversations with them. It's a real aphrodisiac to a lot of women. In my experience, men may not talk as much as women, but if they don't feel pressured to produce a particular response—in other words, if they can relax and be themselves—they will make intimate conversation a regular habit, too. They'll even look forward to it. Whether it's over a glass of wine before dinner or pillow talk after you're in bed, telling your story and really listening to your partner's can be warm and sexy and bonding.

Ask Each Other, What Is a Loving Act?

I often ask my clients, "How do you receive love?" Put another way, "What is love, to you?" One husband, Joe, said, "Loving, to me, is sitting down to the dinner table together." Immediately, his wife, Lulu, became indignant. Didn't he realize that she worked eight hours a day, too? Sometimes she was just too tired to even think about fixing a meal.

I said, "Hold on a minute. All I heard Joe say is that he wanted you both to sit down at the table together. Is that what you meant, Joe?"

It was. Growing up, Joe's family didn't have regular sit-down dinners together. It was something he saw at his friends' houses and envied. It became a symbol of something important to him. I negotiated with Joe and Lulu a plan in which they agreed to take turns getting dinner, whether dinner came by way of takeout, quickly made sandwiches and soup, frozen dinners, leftovers, or a newly cooked dish. The important thing was to have the calm, attentive, and loving ritual of a shared meal.

Fortunately, Joe and Lulu really got into it. Over the next several weeks, they bought candles, place mats and napkins, even a new set of dishes. Joe felt loved, and Lulu got to be a loving spouse. Everybody won.

What feels loving to one partner, may be the opposite to the other. The only way to find out is to ask your partner what is a loving in his eyes alone.

DAY 4: CREATE A ROMANTIC DEN

Good sex can happen anywhere. Well, okay, not *any*where, but in a lot of places. Beds, floors, sofas, dining room tables, countertops, back yards, back seats, front seats, parks, even golf courses late at night. One woman's favorite moment occurred on top of a houseboat at midnight, under a full moon. Many of these settings were impulsive, spontaneous. Not many people actually *plan* to "do it" in Grandma's attic.

Because romance matters to both men and women (even if women talk about it more), it behooves you to work together to create an environment conducive to romantic expression.

Here are some items that can transform an ordinary room into a den of romance:

- Scented candles arranged around the room as the only light
- Extra pillows and special supersoft sheets
- A music player hidden under the bed for sounds that turn you both on
- A movable full-length, freestanding mirror to watch as you touch each other
- Soothing drinks and favorite snacks within reach

As you read this list, notice that each item appeals to one of the five senses. An interesting finding from recent brain research confirms what Aphrodite knew 2,000 years ago: smell is the sense that brings back memories the fastest and most powerfully. That means you can recall a favorite time by re-creating an aroma connected to it, perhaps something sweet and pungent like the jasmine next to the front porch where your husband kissed you good night for the first time.

You can also create new memories by adorning your bedroom or other romantic settings with some favorite scents, whether roses, pine, cinnamon, or lavender. These will then serve both of you as signposts to romance!

DAY 5: FAN THE FLAME

When you were a teenager, you knew a lot about arousal. You had a lot of erotic dreams and daydreams. With a mixture of embarrassment and pride, you monitored the expansion of your breasts or penis. You talked with your friends about how far to go, how far to get, and how far you went/got last Saturday night. You exaggerated or omitted some of the facts. Or maybe you kept all that to yourself.

You were beginning to experience your adult sexuality. It was a scary, confusing, exciting time. And unless you were raised in a vacuum, you eventually had a girlfriend or boyfriend, or just dates you experimented with. You didn't think of it as experimentation, but it was. You were trying on relationships and learning about yourself. And there were probably times when you got very, very hot. Forbidden fruit will do that.

Now that you're a grown-up with your own home and bed, no curfew or foot-tapping parents to put on the brakes, you can go full speed ahead. The problem is, that very fact can lead to boredom. If everything is permitted, where's the thrill of oh-Lord-I-hope-we-don't-get-caught?

Part of the youthful excitement, besides raging hormones and insatiable curiosity, was the realization that you couldn't or mustn't go "all the way." That built-in stop sign allowed you to accelerate right up to it.

Fan the flame, but leave something for later.

Do It Like Teenagers

My suggestion is to re-create those earlier days. Go on a date together, complete with cheeseburgers, Cokes or beer, and hopeful aspirations about making out.

Drive to a secluded spot and turn on the radio. (It might be a good idea to carry a boom box. I once parked so long with a boy, playing the car radio, that the battery finally went dead. Fortunately, the next car over had jumper cables. The phrase "getting jumped" took on new meaning to my date.)

Now start doing what comes naturally. Start with kisses and strokes through your clothes. End up in the back seat, half reclined. You may notice that back seats used to be longer, but on the other hand, maybe you were shorter then.

Once again, my suggestion is leave something for later. Create an exercise in arousal, to remind you of how exciting making out can be. It can be a romantic and arousing end in itself, not just a prelude to sex—although, it is a terrific prelude to sex.

DAY 6: MASSAGE FOR LOVERS

I'm a great believer in giving and receiving massage. I'm not talking about athletic rat-a-tat pounding or deep tissue manipulation. I'm thinking of the kind of nurturing, sensual massage that says "I love you" in a particularly intimate, caring way.

Massage can be done simply as a loving gesture at the end of a long day. In fact, when there's no time for a complete body massage, a hand or foot massage is a great gift. It can be a part of the preamble before sexual activity—as long as you take your time!

So often we consider only the *erogenous zones* as important parts of a partner's body to receive our attention in foreplay, forgetting what we once understood innately as babies. Every part of the body responds to the stimulus of touch. We think immediately of a lover's hands, nipples, genitals, and lips. But what about her forearms, earlobes, brow, scalp, stomach, calves, ankles, and thighs. Each of these parts of the body should receive loving attention during a massage.

How to Give a Relaxation Massage

Although giving a relaxation massage doesn't need a whole lot of preparation, following these steps should lead to a pleasurable experience for both the receiver and the giver. It can serve as a quick stress reliever at the end of a long day, or as an introduction to sex play. It's up to you.

1. Choose a quiet, private place, such as a bedroom or the living room after the kids are asleep.

2. Dim the lights and light some candles. Put on some relaxing music at a low volume.

3. Warm up the room and the massage oil. Drape the bed or massage table with a washable sheet.

4. The person receiving the massage gets nude, lies down on her back, and begins to concentrate on her breathing, inhaling for four seconds and then letting her breath float out.

5. The giver pours a little scented oil into his hands, rubs them together for warmth, then arches his palms an inch over the receiver's face, so she feels the warmth and smells the fragrance.

6. The giver puts his fingertips on her chin and begins to slowly trace the outlines of her facial bones with his hands, as if he were memorizing this precious face to sculpt later.

7. Have the receiver turn over and lie face down. The giver places his oiled palms on the small of her back. Begin to rub her back using both whole hands in gentle, long strokes. Stroke from the base of the back, up toward the neck, and then back down the sides of the back. Do this for at least two minutes.

8. The receiver puts her attention to whatever part of her body is being stroked. Perhaps she even imagines breathing out through that spot. There is no talking unless she wants something a little different: "Please stay there a little longer." "Please stroke a little harder on my feet—they're ticklish."

    Mostly she just softly says "Ahhhhh."

9. The giver gradually increases his pressure as he massages her back and each subsequent area. Knead the flesh around her shoulders and neck, a common place for people who sit at desks all day to hold tension. Follow her muscles across the shoulders and down each arm.

10. Return to the small of the back and use both hands to rub the flesh away from the spine and then back toward it. Keep in rhythm.

11. At the base of the spine, the giver begins stroking downward across the buttocks; then sweeps his hands down each leg several times using a lighter motion.

12. Stroke the calves. Pay particular attention to her feet, rubbing beneath the arch, pulling gently on the toes. When he has finished the massage, the giver turns the receiver back over and gently brings the edges of the sheet over her, to hold in her body warmth. She may fall asleep, which is fine. She can wait till tomorrow night to reciprocate. You have given her a wonderful gift; let her feel the love in your hands.

Go from Relaxing to Exciting

At this point, you should both be feeling fabulous! Of course, there's a very good chance that even a relaxation massage can arouse a lover sexually, particularly when the time, setting, and mood are right.

But if you definitely wish to use massage as foreplay for sex, you can add some different techniques to the mix. The massage begins as described earlier and can go all the way to step 12, or, if you prefer, it can shift to sex somewhere midstream. Here are the essential sensual steps.

1. As you, the giver, work your way down the receiver's back, linger on the buttocks, hips, and inner thighs, working down to the calves and feet.

2. Ask your partner to turn over, and gently rub the stomach and the rest of her lower body. Make your movements long and slow. Your goal now is not to apply pressure as much as it is to build erotic tension. Essentially, you're teasing her, and both of you can enjoy the playfulness of the experience.

3. At the genital area, you have a choice whether to continue building erotic tension as a prelude to intercourse, coming close to her clitoris and perhaps lightly stroking around it. Or you may wish to bring your partner to climax during the massage with direct clitoral stimulation. If you haven't talked about this beforehand, you can whisper the question in her ear while staying in a playful mode. If you plan to have intercourse, you can join your partner right there on the floor or bed. Or you may wish to shower together first to remove the oil. If you head to the shower, be sure to continue playfully touching each other while soaping up and rinsing.

If sex is on the menu without pausing for a shower or a change of location, your intention will show. Nipples and genitals will get stroked, lips will touch lips, and heat will rise. When you couple (no pun intended) your sense of touch with skill about where and how you touch, you are on your way to sexual delight.

DAY 7: PLAY A FANTASY GAME

Sexual fantasies are like book and movie genres. Some fantasies look like historic romances, with swashbuckling pirates, bluebloods, and damsels in distress. Others resemble horror shows with sexy vampires and ladies trapped in dungeons. Of course, there are other fantasies that could be straight out of a porn movie.

Likewise, your own personal fantasies come with a wide range of characters, costumes, plots, and emotions. The important thing to remember is that they're all fantasies, meaning they're not real unless you want to make them so. And if you do, there are ways to make them safe, pleasurable, and harmless.

All of us have fantasies, even if you don't think you do. They happen while you dream at night or while you sit (daydreaming) in your cubicle during the day. Men and women have them, albeit usually different kinds.

Some sexual fantasies feature situations and scenes you might someday want to actually act out with your current partner. Others remain strictly fantasies, meaning you wouldn't want them to occur anytime, anywhere outside of the privacy of your imagination. The latter category may include fantasies you may wish to share, meaning *tell* to your real-life sexual partner. Indeed, many such fantasies, perhaps too intense for real life, can add a welcome erotic edge to a couple's lovemaking when verbalized in the heat of passion.

A very common female sex fantasy, perhaps the most common, is where a man "takes" his woman, unexpectedly sweeping her off into erotic paradise. Here's one you can try, with a simple mail carrier or other delivery person costume, or simply with your imaginations at play.

The Mailman Cometh

There's a knock on the door. "Package, ma'am." The woman goes to answer it, and standing on her porch is her fiancé, looking severe and wearing what looks like a postal worker's uniform. He shoves her inside and proceeds to kiss her roughly. He pulls off her sweater, then her slacks and panties, tosses her onto the sofa, and ravishes her. It is hot! He then leaves as unexpectedly as he appeared.

Later, when he gets home, he asks innocently, "So, honey, how'd your day go?"

"Oh, same ol' same ol'," she answers airily.

They never speak of the incident again, but she conjures up the memory when she's self-pleasuring. Is this a safe fantasy to play out? Of course, if it's your partner as the mailman, and you're both game to play out a "Take Me" fantasy. Masterful (not cruel) seduction is, without question, a favorite fantasy for millions of women. Author Margaret Mitchell knew exactly what she was doing in *Gone With The Wind* when she made Rhett Butler confident and masterful.

CHOOSE A SAFE WORD

Lovers who want to try out fantasies involving force or gentle restraints should choose a *safe word* before they begin. This is a word (never *no* or *stop*) that means "Stop immediately." A safe word like *pineapple* or *computer* leaves no room for confusion about one partner's intent to stop or take a break from your sex play. A safe word allows both of you to let go and enjoy the fantasy.

Hey, men, are you getting confused? Maybe you've been working on becoming more sensitive and more emotionally accessible, and now here I am talking about your getting masterful. Is this a double message? Not really, because all of us can be gentle or powerful at different times and in different ways.

Tenderness is sweet and sexy. Then there are other times when a woman wants you to take over and be in charge, still considerate of how she likes it, but also masterful.

Ironically, the more assertive and executive the woman is in business, often the more she appreciates a lover with confidence and sureness—not turning into a cave man, just being, well, authoritative. And she might enjoy giving little eyelash-flutter, just for fun.

Of course, there will be other times when she wants to be the one on top, in more ways than one. We've all got lots and lots of gears and fantasies. Dig into your dreams and daydreams to find new ways to express your desire. Talk about these different parts of you with your partner. Choose which roles to play out and which to leave to the safety of your imagination. Mine your fantasies to spice up your sex life.

Fantasies are a sure-fire way to keep sex sizzling, especially in long-term marriages.

DETOUR: NO SEX FOR THE WEARY

I call these *detours* on the way to *Sizzling Sex.* They may be frustrating, but they're not serious roadblocks. Solutions can be found to these challenges with some simple guidance, usually without professional intervention.

Let's begin with a common scenario in many a modern marriage, particularly in those with young children and a stay-at-home mom, or in households with two extremely busy working parents. This scenario involves a woman who no longer considers herself sexually appealing. Her husband becomes frustrated by his wife's sexual withdrawal and what he perceives as her emotional neediness without giving him the kind of attention she used to shine his way. Both partners end up feeling abandoned.

Here's an example. Annie is the stay-at-home mother of two young children: Sam, age two-and-a-half, and Becca, five months. Becca mostly sleeps through the night, but not always, and Sam knows lots of ways to push Mommy's buttons, day and night.

Annie's day starts before dawn (often after several get-ups) and doesn't get a break all day, except when both kids are napping. Instead of resting then, she scurries around trying to get caught up on *anything.* Grocery shopping can be grueling, too, with Annie having to corral Sam and keep a constant eye on Becca's carrier in the kiddie seat of the grocery cart. Of course, Sam may well throw one of his dramatic tantrums when Annie won't buy him yet another of the toys the store displays at his eye level.

Husband Brad helps with the kids when he gets home and takes some of the nighttime alarms. But Brad can do only so much and still get up for work, and last through an eight-hour day. He sometimes wonders what Annie does all day, but he rarely complains aloud.

Being on call 24 hours a day leads Annie to a state of near-permanent exhaustion and takes a heavy toll on her self-image. Every day she looks down at what used to be her flat belly and sees a pooch she knows will never completely disappear. Her breasts are tender and so is her self-image. Gone are the days of facial masks, bubble baths, and workouts.

At night all Annie wants to do is prop up in bed and read a few pages until the magazine or book droops and so do her eyelids.

Brad often hopes for some lovemaking, but once again Annie is out like a light. Frankly, at this moment in her life, sex is just one more thing on her to-do list, and Brad senses it.

Annie used to make Brad the beacon of her life, but now she has a hard time summoning up interest in "How was your day, honey?" Brad tries to be a good sport, but he's feeling deserted, abandoned, and unloved. If your marriage resembles Brad and Annie's, please don't lose hope.

Some Survival Tips for the Sleepless *and* Sexless

Intimacy is sharing exactly how you feel with your partner, not pretending to be something or someone you're not. Here are some ideas to bring real intimacy back to your relationship during tough times.

- Cut yourselves some slack. Realize that "this, too, shall pass."
- Have honest conversations; share your feelings of exhaustion, frustration, or abandonment.
- Listen; don't judge. Your objective is simply to be a sympathetic witness for each other during this challenging time. In other words, remember you're "on the same side," the side of your relationship.
- Pick a few activities from the *Sizzling Sex* program. Do a bit of self-prep, talk, romance, or play a fantasy game.

Most of all, take it easy. Sex is fun, not work!

Notice that although I encourage couples in this situation to accept the limitations of their situation, and to avoid blame or acting out, I still encourage them to make time to be a couple, alone.

How to Keep the Embers of Desire Glowing

Much as we might all wish to check into a hotel for a month to focus entirely on the *Sizzling Sex,* real life has a way of intruding. That's why you have to practice being a juggler with time for intimacy always one of the balls you keep up in the air. Here are some concrete things you can do to not "drop the ball."

Make Some Time for Each Other

I know, I know, it's too much work to even think about going out on a date with your spouse. Please hear me. Couples who find they are chronically overstretched for time and energy are in danger of losing emotional touch with each other permanently. To prevent this unwanted outcome, you simply *must* figure out a way to spend some quality time, alone. You can call it a date, or not. Just do it!

Your time alone can take place on a Saturday night at home with wine and cheese and romantic music or, if you're very lucky, a night out at a restaurant while Grandma or a sitter looks after the kids.

Sample the *Sizzling Sex* Program

You don't have to do the whole thing all at once. Try some sense-awakening exercises together, massage her feet, light some candles in the bedroom, answer a revealing question as if you were speaking for each other: "What thrilled you most as a child?" or "What does love feel like to you?" It will help keep you connected emotionally and sensually.

Cuddle First

Many couples benefit from regular physical contact, at least a cuddle, before bed, even if it needs to come as soon as the kids are down, at least for the first round. And remember, men, for many a woman, lovemaking doesn't start with desire. It comes after her arousal, and women can be aroused by romance, stroking, even just looking deeply into her eyes.

An understanding of each other's current frustrations *and* hopes for more sexual intimacy in the future can go a long way toward easing the present tensions in your relationship.

Chapter 5

WAYS TO EXCITE YOUR LOVER

Seduction is a fine art. Think of Casanova, the preeminent flirt of Europe. What was his secret? By all reports, he *paid attention* to his beloved, in every conceivable manner. He listened and looked closely, brought flowers to arouse her senses, sent messages of love—and he took his time, never rushing what could be enjoyed slowly. In these hectic days when time is money and shortcuts rule, how can you recapture the spirit of the great lovers of history?

Over the next six days, you'll discover how to excite and please your lover (and yourself) by going back to the same basics: preparing your bodies for passion, arousing the senses, letting your hands caress and your lips ignite, and reminding each other of your still-burning desire when apart, all the time moving ever so slowly to a blissful finale on Day 12.

DAY 8: PAMPER YOUR BODY

Today your assignment is to rejuice and rejoice in yourself!

Pamper *yourself* to excite your partner? *Yes.* There's nothing sexier than self-confidence—an enlivened body and a sense of your own self-worth. After all, if you don't find yourself sexy, why should your lover? The purpose of today's self-pampering exercise is to make you feel so good about you, inside and out, that you exude sexiness.

A Bath Fit for a King or Queen

An easy way to pamper yourself into a state of hypersexiness is to indulge in the privacy of your own bath. Now, you may wonder why you need to be told to do something as simple and natural as bathing. Think about it—when was the last time you took an hour to explore your own sensual pleasure in a tub of silky, steamy water? I'm not talking about a quick shower while someone is pounding on the bathroom door wanting to know when you'll be done. Enough said. Here are the essentials.

- Leave that day's worries and self-doubts behind.
- Tape a "Do Not Disturb" note on the bathroom door.
- Give yourself a 30-minute minimum of uninterrupted bathroom time.
- Fill the tub with hot water, as hot as you can stand it.
- Dim the electric lights; light candles.
- Put a few drops of essential oils in the water; lavender is especially good for relaxing, rose for enlivening.
- Play some favorite calming music.
- Add bubble bath for heightened aroma or bath salts for enhanced muscle relaxation.
- Don't forget a pillow for your head.

Now step into your solo sensual bath, paying attention to all your senses. Notice the temperature; the smell of the oils, shampoo, and soap; the sensual feeling of the water; the little splashing sounds in the tub.

- Turn your focus to your skin, stomach, and legs; apply soap and wash lovingly with a washcloth or bath brush.

- Bathe s-l-o-w-l-y. Notice your toes, which are overdue for some appreciation; same with your knees, belly, armpits, all your utilitarian body parts. Stay out of your head; go into your sensual body.

- Use positive self-talk to better appreciate your body and yourself as a sexual being. (What I love about my body …. What I love about my sexuality ….)

- As the water cools down, step out of the tub, towel off, lovingly smooth lotion onto your still-warm skin, and retreat to your bedroom.

- Take another 20 minutes to lie nude on your bed, breathing deeply, loving and appreciating your body—the only one you've got this time around!

As you get up, vow to keep all the positive feelings as part of who you are from this point on.

DAY 9: LOVING TALK

Today you and your partner are going to take between 30 and 60 minutes *just to talk with each other.* Not about the kids, or chores, or bills, or jobs. The key to loving talk time is to make this a special slot in your week. When the two of you find the best day or evening time to schedule it (and, yes, I mean *schedule* it), you'll ideally do it at least once a week from here on, to create and sustain a deep, ongoing intimacy in your relationship.

If you are habitually early risers, you may decide to try your first loving talk time on a Saturday or Sunday morning before you jump out of bed and start your errands. Alternately, you may attach a half-hour of loving talk to your weekly "date night," or give this activity a night all its own.

Women tell me every day that they wish their partners would have intimate conversations with them. It's a real aphrodisiac to a lot of women. Whether it's over a glass of wine before dinner or pillow talk after you're in bed, telling your story and really listening to your partner's can be warm and sexy.

Make it a time for lazy dream-making about your future together or remembering good times you've enjoyed in the past. You can get things started with questions or statements like these:

- Where was our first kiss?
- I first realized I loved you when ….
- What I love most about you is ….
- I think you're sexy because ….

Communication can begin with other people's words and music. One couple keeps a book of song lyrics by the bed, and sometimes they open it and read familiar songs to each other. I know it sounds corny, but it certainly works for them. They go from lazy smiles of remembrance to arched eyebrows, from come-hither looks to sexy kisses, all the way to happy afterglows.

The secret of loving talk is to make it more about the process than the content of your conversation. Be creative in finding the right channel to send on—and, remember, a channel is particular to the person sending or receiving the communication.

Male and Female Talk Styles

Because I am a great believer in finding commonality between the sexes, I generally refrain from making sweeping generalizations about the differences between us—that whole Mars and Venus thing. At the same time, I agree that there *is* some dissimilarity in how males and females communicate. If you factor these differences into your loving talk times, you'll both be happier with your conversations, whether they take place in the bedroom or at the breakfast table.

For starters, men and women tend to talk for different reasons, and they often process information differently. It's a mind/body thing. Brain scientists tell us that women really do hear more than men. (Your disagreements about how loud is too loud for the TV and stereo are one good example of this.) Conversely, men really do see and perceive visual stimuli more clearly than women do (think maps). The implications of these neurological differences are twofold. Women are more verbally oriented, while men operate and make decisions more from what they see. Women like to talk things out; men, less so.

Women talk as a way of connecting, certainly with each other, and if a partner is willing and available, with him, too. Women talk to relieve anxiety and to think out loud, without necessarily looking for an immediate solution to a problem.

Because women are more inclined to communicate when upset, a woman's silence often means more than a man's. Men, if you haven't heard from your partner in a long while (and only you can decide what's longer than usual), it can mean she's feeling shut down or alienated.

Men talk to exchange information, solve problems, or, with other men, sometimes to compete. When anxious or angry, men often seek solitude rather than talk, at least as an immediate response. So women, if your man has been out in the garage or has been waxing his car for several hours, he's more likely to be processing things his way than feeling alienated from you.

Of course, each of us is a unique combination of what we define, both biologically and culturally, as masculine and feminine traits. Your husband may be more of a talker than your girlfriend's more taciturn spouse. You may be the more circumspect one in your marriage. Your job is to discover how your sweetheart best receives what you have to say and adjust your choice of words, tone, and timing to best reach him. To do this, you must put yourself in his shoes and find the best channel for your loving talk.

Same Desire, Different Channels

A man and a woman may both want intimacy or connection with each other but may use different words to ask for what they want. See if you can guess who's asking each of the following questions, a man or woman.

- Hey, can we talk?
- Hey, want to fool around?

Right. The first speaker was probably female, the second male.

Besides styles, timing is important. The two of you may have to negotiate which comes first in your loving talk times, sex or conversation. Both are important and often serve as reflections of each other, but don't let the differences in your styles obstruct what you both want: an intimate connection.

For the purposes of today's assignment (Day 9), I recommend that you delay sexual gratification, at least until later this week (Day 12). Trust me, there's a method to my madness.

Along with better, more lustful sex when that time comes, you'll gain another benefit from your regular loving talk sessions. By committing to special times when you focus exclusively on the quality of your intimate communication, you'll find the rest of your daily interactions infused with tenderness and affection. Many couples like to discreetly bring the intimacy of loving talk or lovemaking from the bedroom into their everyday humdrum existence by using special nicknames when they talk to each other around the house or on the telephone. Raunchy or sweet, I'll leave the choice of such terms of endearment entirely up to you.

DAY 10: CARESSES AND KISSES

Ladies and gentlemen, I have an announcement: loving strokes and deep kisses are not simply pit stops on the way to sexual intercourse. Too often we reduce these vital aspects of human sensuality to mere stepping-stones on our way elsewhere.

Today's exercise, designed to help you rediscover the joy of physically connecting with your partner (short of intercourse, for now), comes in two parts.

First, I want you to keep your clothes on. Whether you call it necking, petting, making out, or whatever, your assignment is to spend at least 20 minutes kissing, holding, and caressing, with all your clothes in place. It doesn't matter where—the sofa is a nice place to start.

The fact that you've agreed to not have sex yet and are not goal oriented can actually liberate you. Remember how turned on you used to get when you were a teenager, not yet ready to go "All the way"? Somehow that forbidden fruit aspect of making out allows you to really feel your own desire, lust, goose bumps … whatever you'd like to call that longing for each other.

The Art of the Kiss

Most of the women and a great number of men I've counseled over the years have said the same thing about arousal: there's nothing like a good kiss to get you going, a soft-lipped, moist, searching kiss. If you don't like the way your partner kisses, show her or him what you prefer. There are only a few ground rules for this exercise: no sloppy over-wet kisses, no ravaging tongue that tries to reach the tonsils—just sexy kisses.

Lips are some of the most sensitive parts of the body, and soft little exploratory kisses can tease, arouse, and finally inflame. Some people love to have their necks nuzzled and earlobes gently sucked. Some people even like to have tongues stuck in their ears. Others think it's revolting. As always, pay attention to what your honey likes.

Kiss, kiss, kiss. Kiss softly with your lips gently closed, like children do. Then touch the other's lips with your tongue, first in the center, then all across and back again. Finally, let your tongue enter your lover's mouth. Experiment with shy kisses, powerful kisses, long ones, light and teasing ones. Not too wet, please, and not dry. Just right.

At this point, you might be saying, "Hey, we've been married for 13 years. What's to learn?" The answer is, a lot.

Caress Each Other

Now for part two, when you explore kisses and caresses in a more explicit way. This one may be especially appealing to you men. Still focusing on sensuality only, have one of you lie down, first on the stomach and then the back, allowing your partner to caress your naked body in a way that he or she thinks might feel good to you.

Unlike massage, the goal is not to relieve muscular tension, but simply to pay loving attention to your partner's body, without sex on the agenda. Avoid genitals at this time. Keep it slow and sensual. Become reacquainted with the range of pleasurable sensations through touch, to learn about your own and your partner's pleasure and, ultimately, arousal.

When you are the receiver, give feedback about what feels good, how you like being touched, and what you'd like different. Tenderly say things like, "That's nice. Do that some more." or "I'm a little ticklish there, I need deeper pressure." or "Slower … oh, that's it." Your only responsibility is to put your attention on where your partner's hands are on your body, on the good feelings you get. You are totally the recipient of this nurturing.

When you are the giver, pay attention not only to the pleasure you are giving, but also to the pleasure you experience in stroking your lover's body. What do you particularly enjoy? Explore your beloved's body as if you've never seen it before. Perhaps you'd like to try sucking on a clean little toe or running your tongue down your lover's spine, paying respectful attention to the feedback you get.

Be clear from the start that you are merely awakening the sensual part of your relationship, without the goal of having sex. Even though you may become aroused, don't act on it sexually. You are using this exercise as a trust experience, without the possibility of performance. In a few days, you may decide to include genitals and later may move to a sexual level. But don't undermine your efforts to thoroughly explore the sensual before sexualizing the experience.

The Miraculous Breast

Let's take a new look at breasts and nipples. If you haven't seen it, go rent a video of the movie *Big*, about a boy who wishes he were a grown-up and wakes up to find he's still a boy but is in a man's body.

In one scene, he sees a woman's breast for the first time. He reaches out his hand and gently touches its side, then cups it in his hand as if it is the most amazing, miraculous thing he's ever seen (which it probably is).

That's a great way to start with breasts. Soon, though, you can do more grown-up stuff, like tonguing and sucking nipples, *gently* nipping with your teeth, and *gently* squeezing and kissing them. You are appreciating her breasts, not grabbing. Women generally do not like to be grabbed—anywhere. Believe me.

Many men have extremely erogenous nipples, too. Try the lick-suck-nip action on him, and feel his temperature go up about 10 degrees.

Even though their bodies may respond alike in many ways, men and women often experience arousal differently. With men desire usually comes first, then the turn-on, some foreplay, intercourse, and orgasm. Women have lived by that model for centuries, but now we're realizing that pleasure doesn't necessarily work that way for them. Women like to be in the moment, to savor it, to enjoy everything that's pleasurable without wondering what next. Women often have more intense orgasms if they don't feel *The Big O* as the goal. They love to enjoy the luscious trip.

DAY 11: SEXY MESSAGES

Today we have a brief tutorial on the art of sending sexy messages. You may wonder, why send a message when you'll see your partner in a matter of hours? First, to let him know you're thinking of him. More important, to inspire his anticipation of your next sexual encounter, now just a day away.

I invite you to take a moment and remember your early courtship. One delightful aspect of that infatuation period was the exchange of notes, e-mails, voice-mail messages, and long, late conversations. Every contact added something to your budding romance: the flowers delivered to your office on Valentine's Day, the first time she signed a card "Love ...," his first phone message that began "Hey gorgeous, it's me ..." and ended "Love you."

You can recapture much of that early delight right now. Send your lover a seductive message before your Inner Critic starts trying to talk you out of it, saying you're too old, too long married, too established as a couple for such nonsense. What a crock! Tell that monkey chatter to get lost.

Part of the fun of these messages is the not knowing, the surprise element. Another is your heightened anticipation of what might happen when you see each other again. Once you've recaptured that lovely feeling of courtship, there's no reason to abandon flirtatious contact in favor of "Please buy milk on the way home" or "I'm working late tonight," those (let's face it) awfully dull messages that pepper most established couples' communications. You have every reason to continue sharing reminders of your attraction for each other, especially when you're not there in person to say it with a wink of an eye or with a quick kiss.

A sexy message from your lover can provide the pizzazz in your day, a reason to hurry home from the office. It can also function as a delicious turn-on.

My Sexy Message Tutorial

Whichever medium you choose—voice mail, post, a note tucked in her suit jacket pocket or taped to the steering wheel, or an e-mail (make sure it's for her eyes only)—take the following steps before you commit words to the page or screen, or begin talking "after the beep."

- Get in a playful mood; put aside chores or work for a couple of minutes.
- Picture your lover at his most alluring.
- Now imagine he's thinking of you in the same way, and about your last passionate evening together.
- Separated by geography and responsibilities, you pine for each other. Feel the longing. It's true that separation makes the heart grow fonder.
- Say or write what you want *from him,* or what you want to *give her.*
- Deliver the message as an invitation for a special evening.

I guarantee your lover will come home, or meet you at the appointed place, turned on and ready for love and romance, or whatever you two have in mind.

DAY 12: GOING ALL THE WAY ... SLOWLY

Tonight, at last, you're going to have that very special date. If you've followed the *Sizzling Sex* program as I've laid it out, you've patiently waited until today to *go all the way.*

So have your date. Whether you go out or stay at home, make it special: luscious food, slow dancing, plenty of flirting. You're becoming lovers again, maybe more than ever.

Over the course of the evening, you've been laughing, talking, play-fully touching hands, forearms, cheeks—and also letting the silences simply "be" while the sexual energy between you builds. When the preliminaries are over, you can relocate to your bedroom or hotel room, any place that's private and decidedly romantic, to begin the evening's sexual encounter.

Foreplay

Look at the word *foreplay* a minute. *Fore* means "before." *Play* means "play." It's before intercourse, but all of it is part of making love. And as you saw when you made out like teenagers again, love play does not have to be the intro to intercourse. It can be wonderful all by itself. Give it the time to be wonderful tonight, too.

Provide plenty of time for kissing. Sadly, foreplay is the part of sex that tends to get left behind in long-term relationships. No more. Let your lips, mouth, fingers, and palms get reacquainted with your partner's face, neck, ears, eyelids, and head. Study them as if you're memorizing those features for the first time.

Undress slowly, perhaps removing each other's clothing a piece at a time. As you disrobe, keep touching each other. Turn each other around, discovering exposed parts anew: back, buttocks, stomach, thighs, neck, and feet. When you lie down, naked, keep touching, stroking the other's torso up and down with fingers and palms extended.

When the time is right, stroke penis and vulva until you are both very aroused. Have intercourse as slowly as you can. Make it last. Try putting a pillow beneath the buttocks of the person on the bottom. Move in that timeless rocking motion, "like your back ain't got no bone."

Secrets of Intimate Talk

Remember to keep communicating during intercourse, with and without words, staying connected to your partner on every level. It's important to know the words that turn each of you on, or signal your intentions or desires before or during intercourse.

Those words may well be different for each of you. Some women are turned off hearing their men talk "dirty"—but trust me, many others absolutely love hearing "Oh, baby, I'm gonna …." Many a man gets turned on by saying these words to his woman, and even more by hearing "Oh, baby, I love it when you …." He may want to hear you talk erotically about his cock, his balls—the heat of sexuality is no time for clinical terms. Such talk can give sex an edge, a sense of new energy. It's also a way to get over shyness in fantasy role-playing, something we explore several more times in the *Sizzling Sex* program.

Here are some do's and don'ts for loving talk during or immediately after your lovemaking:

- Don't speak negatively of your own body or your partner's.
- Do guide him to satisfy you with questions and statements such as "Does this feel good?" and "Oh, do that some more."
- Don't be silent.
- Do express your satisfaction with groans, coos, moans, whatever feels natural to you. Words are not essential, but communication is.
- Don't say "No" immediately to your partner's suggestion of a new position or sexual technique that might push your comfort level. It's perfectly okay to say, "Maybe later, I'd like to think about it."
- Don't bring up difficult issues for discussion.
- Do make declarations of your love and sexual thrills.

Rejoice! Your sexual relationship is officially rekindled. Now let's see how you can keep it spicy.

DAY 13: SPICING IT UP

Now that the spark has been relit, it's important not to fall back into complacency. This is not the time to go back to the same restaurant every date night, or to get stuck on the same tried-and-true sexual position(s). To give your reawakened sexuality a permanent home in your relationship, you must keep those embers of desire fired up—not all the time, of course, but often enough to retain the sizzle.

On this Day 13 of the *Sizzling Sex* program, I want you to take out your journal and allow your impressions of the last 12 days of sexual reawakening to roam freely. Then write down the completions to these statements, without censoring your thoughts or feelings. Make room for new sexual fantasies, too.

- The thing my partner did before our sex that turned me on the most was ….
- What I liked best in our lovemaking is ….
- What I wish I'd said/asked for during intercourse to make it more enjoyable/exciting was ….
- If my partner was to say what he or she wants more or less of in our sex, I think it would be ….
- Another sexual position I'd like us to try is ….

Then consider and write down your answers to these questions.

- How do I feel different about myself now that we've resumed/enhanced our sexual relationship?
- How has our sex and/or the relationship changed after 12 days of doing this program?

Reflect on these answers solo at first. If you choose to share them with your partner, be careful about your tone. Use I-messages, not you-messages. Ask for what you want. Own your feelings. Suggest things you can try in your future lovemaking to make the sex better, the relationship stronger.

DETOUR: BODY IMAGE

Robert and Jeannie are a couple in their early 40s who, when they first came to me for sex therapy, hadn't had sexual relations in over five years. After the birth of their second child, Jeannie couldn't lose the 30 pounds she'd gained during her pregnancy, and her morale was in bad shape. Meanwhile, Robert felt frustrated, lonely, and unloved. The strain of his wanting sex and her repeatedly saying "No" had taken its toll on the relationship. He rarely asked anymore. But he didn't have to; Jeannie said, "It's always in the background." On weekends, the two dealt with the household and kids, rarely doing anything alone as a couple.

"The problem is, I don't feel sexy," Jeannie said after Robert shared his feelings.

"But I still think you're sexy," he said. "Isn't that enough?" Jeannie looked away as tears started to fall down her cheeks. "You're just saying that," she said. Clearly, it was *not* enough.

Robert and Jeannie still loved each other and wanted to stay together, and they were way too young to give up sex. What could they do?

Many women who no longer like their bodies refuse to believe their husbands still want them sexually. They have made the error of mistaking their current figure for their body. They feel loss, grief, and frustration. Since they can't see themselves as desirable, they mistrust their man's reassurances.

First, I needed to help Robert and Jeannie realize that their situation was understandable and not unusual. "We can get past this" was an enormous relief to them both.

They needed to see clearly what was happening, have empathy for each other, and come to a clear decision to fix what was wrong. Jeannie needed to come to terms with a body that had been altered by childbirth but was by no means over the hill. "A real man prefers a woman to a girl," I said, and Robert's heartfelt "Amen" made Jeannie laugh and relax for the first time in a long while. She had been telling herself scary stories, convinced Robert would look elsewhere now that she was billowy.

They made an ironclad agreement to nurture their relationship in all the ways we've covered in Days 1 to 12 of this *Sizzling Sex* program. As they moved through the program, they learned more about each other's feelings. Jeannie gradually became more confident and decided to lose the weight for herself, not for Robert or their relationship. Robert learned that while he couldn't fix her insecurity, he could just go on loving her and also courting her a bit more. They realized how they had both been lonely for each other, and they began to reach out to each other in new ways.

With honest communication and several weeks of working at creating romance, making time alone, and playing with nondemand sensual touch, Robert and Jeannie gradually rekindled their emotional and sexual connection and resumed a satisfying sex life.

Like all good things, healthy, sizzling sex takes a real commitment to yourself and the relationship, a willingness to move through uncomfortable feelings, and good old-fashioned effort. It also helps when the partners make time for more fun and more play, and stay open to the flow of life changes. "This, too, shall pass" beats "The sky is falling!" just about every time.

Chapter 6

PLEASURE FOR BODY/MIND

The brain is your body's most sexually sensitive organ, so it follows that as you and your lover touch hands or brush lips, your brains go to work sending messages from head to toe, enriching and expanding on these initial physical sensations.

One way you can enhance your pleasure is by attuning your physical senses and thoughts to go beyond your prior sexual expectations. What does that mean for you? No more ho-hum sex!

In this third week of the *Sizzling Sex* program, you learn the fine points of male and female sexual anatomy, exploring pleasure zones that can transport you beyond your customary erotic experience. We put just as much attention on your mind: how to tease each other with exotic dance and surprise with seductively playful mind games. With this advanced knowledge, you can move into the stratosphere of erotic potential.

Day 14: Work Your Magic Muscle

Before you try today's activity, here's an interesting historical footnote. Back in the 1940s, a physician named Dr. Arnold Kegel devised an exercise to help women get back their muscle tone after childbirth. Though his purpose was to help patients get better bladder control, there was another fortuitous outcome: their sex lives got much better!

I'm certain that courtesans and other sexually knowledgeable women attained this skill centuries before Dr. Kegel was around, but we can thank him for making it generally acceptable and accessible.

The Kegel exercise strengthens and tones the PC muscle (pubococcygeal muscle) that controls the pelvic area in women and men. Although the PC muscle is interwoven with and surrounded by four other sets of pelvic muscles, it is the master muscle, the sling that supports the entire pelvic area. When it's weak, bladder control and vaginal muscles are weakened. Doing Kegels makes the vagina (and penis!) stronger. Kegels can help you reach orgasm, make your orgasms more intense, and enable the woman to s-q-u-e-e-z-e her partner's penis, which is exciting for them both.

His and Hers Kegels

Men, this is the muscle you use to make your erect penis jump and your anus pull upward. The more you do Kegels, the better you will be able to delay and control your orgasm. Many men report that these exercises seem to make erections easier and increase the intensity of their orgasm. Also, performing several voluntary contractions as you feel yourself getting closer to ejaculation can help you last longer, which means Kegels can be a great antidote to premature ejaculation. Practice until you can hang a handkerchief on your erect penis and make it bob up and down—a new kind of sex play.

Women, I realize this may be one area of fitness you've never thought of, but it's important. As you get older, and especially if you've had pregnancies, your pelvic floor muscles can get out of shape. Whether or not you've had children, doing Kegels regularly can revolutionize your sexual enjoyment and do wonders for your self-esteem. Believe me, Kegels can do more for your self-confidence than all the sit-ups or crunches in your exercise regimen.

Doing Kegels also helps prevent the embarrassing mini tinkle when you cough or sneeze hard, or hear a particularly hilarious joke. Kegel exercises help reduce all kinds of pelvic floor problems, make for easier and more gratifying orgasms, and help prevent vaginal and uterine prolapse.

How to Do Kegels

A Kegel is simply the contraction and release of your PC muscles. You can do these anywhere, and no one will know. The trick is to know *how* to do them.

First, you need to isolate the feeling of a Kegel contraction. The best way, for both men and women, is to stop and start your urine flow. When you "suck up" to stop peeing, you are contracting your PC muscle. When you relax the muscle, your urine flows out again. In a short while, you will be able to isolate it further so that you can flex and release your PC even when you have a full bladder.

This stop-and-start-your-urine experiment is only to become familiar with the muscle, though; it's not to be done regularly when urinating.

Now let's start Kegeling.

1. Lie on the floor or bed with your knees bent and the soles of your feet facing each other. You may want to put a rolled pillow under each knee in the beginning.

2. Relax your stomach and vaginal muscles. Then squeeze your vagina, using the muscle you discovered when you stopped your urine.

3. Hold the contraction for six seconds. Don't tighten your butt or stomach muscles.

4. Relax completely for another six seconds, and then repeat 10 times.

Start off doing Kegels just a few at a time throughout your day. As your muscle gets stronger, you'll hold each contraction longer and more strongly. Begin with a set three times a day, then gradually increase to as often as you like. Don't be impatient. It may take three or four weeks of regular Kegels before you see a difference, but believe me, it's worth the trip.

Advanced Kegeling

Your goal is to work up to three sets of 10 a day, then three sets three times a day. Once you get the hang of it, you can do these contractions while you're driving, watching TV, or any other time you want to. In the "advanced" version, you hold the squeeze for 10 seconds; then make a fast, harder squeeze; and then release for 10 seconds.

If you get sore doing them, back off a bit. Like any muscle, the PC can get fatigued.

Women, to monitor your progress, put a finger into your vagina and feel the grasp when you do your Kegel contraction.

Men, if you put a finger into your rectum, you can feel the same grip.

You're doing the Kegels wrong if your buttocks, legs, or stomach muscles get tired. Use the inserted finger technique to check out whether you've mastered them.

Questions About Kegeling

Q: What if I get turned on?

A: Actually, that often happens. In fact, many people incorporate Kegels into lovemaking and self-pleasuring, and find that their orgasms are terrific.

Q: My vagina is already painfully tight. Why would I want to make it even tighter?

A: Amazingly, toning the PC muscle can help ease painful intercourse. *Relaxing* the muscle completely is as important as contracting it, and a woman can't always tell whether she has released all the way. When one of my women clients is experiencing pain during intercourse and her gynecologist has ruled out any organic reason for it, I sometimes refer her to a physical therapist who specializes in pelvic muscle biofeedback. Just a few sessions with her physical therapist can instruct her not only in how firmly she is contracting, but also in how to completely let go.

Q: Can this really improve my sex life?

A: If both of you have been practicing your Kegels, you can add a great new sex technique. Once the penis is in the vagina, instead of the old in-and-out thrusting, just lie there and take turns contracting your PC muscles. When she contracts, she is squeezing and hugging his penis. When he contracts, he is tapping the "ceiling" of her vagina and may even be nudging her G-spot; more about the G-spot on Day 16.

Remember, the couple that Kegels together, plays together!

DAY 15: ORAL SEX—WHAT YOU LIKE BEST OR MIGHT WANT TO TRY

Sometimes it seems the world is divided into two camps: those who absolutely love to give and/or receive oral sex, and those who avoid it at all costs. I am not looking for converts. However, if you already like it, I can show you how to like it more. And if you don't, you might want to try a couple of ideas to see if you change your mind.

Men, as a rule, *love* being on the receiving end of oral sex. However, some men avoid giving oral pleasure to their partners (technically, cunnilingus, more colloquially, "going down on her"). A few may be turned off by pubic hair or vaginal odors, and others may not be confident of their oral sex skills, so they opt out rather than risk not pleasing the woman.

While some women don't like receiving or giving oral sex (technically, fellatio, in colloquial terms, "giving head" or "blow job"), this number is often exaggerated. A recent *Redbook Report on Female Sexuality* found that only 6 percent said they didn't like oral sex, while 62 percent said they like it a lot, and for 26 percent it was simply okay.

Let's start afresh, literally.

I am assuming that you both come to bed reasonably soon after a bath. I mean, pretty recently, not *days* later. A soapy washcloth or toilet tissue works fine, but be sure to rinse thoroughly to avoid get-ting an irritation.

Let's say you have given each other some deep, soft, luscious kisses. Sent that eye-twinkle back and forth. S-l-o-w-l-y undressed yourselves or each other. Now you're on the bed, hugging, stroking, caressing, licking, nibbling, holding, massaging, or whatever you like to do. Your arousal is heating up. You can feel electricity along your skin.

Men, spread your lady's legs and look at her vulva. It doesn't take much imagination to see why it's been likened to a flower. Now kiss the little hollow where her leg joins her body. Now, the other one. Nuzzle in her pubic hair a little. Spread her petals and, with a flat, wet tongue, lap her a couple of times, like a cat lapping milk.

Did you enjoy that? If not, okay. Nobody says you have to. Did she enjoy it? If she grew up with a heavy dose of "it's nasty" program-ming, maybe she didn't. But it was worth a try, wasn't it?

Women, take your partner's penis in your hand and gently stroke it up and down. That skin is the finest fabric in the world. It's like silk. And that foam-rubber head is designed to make you comfortable when it slides into you. Now give the shaft some little teasing kisses while you move your hand up and down.

You can keep kissing the head. Is it a little wet? That's okay; it proba-bly tastes like tears, slightly salty. (This is called pre-ejaculate. It does contain semen, so if you do not want to get pregnant, you'll want to get to the condom-fitting part of sex play before intercourse.) If you want to continue kissing and sucking his penis, enjoy. If you don't, then stop at the point where it starts to not be fun for you. Believe me, you have already given him a thrill.

What if he comes in your mouth? I suggest you taste his semen and see if that's okay with you. If it isn't, you can work a deal where he tells you when he's getting close and you lift your mouth.

See? That wasn't scary, was it? If the answer is "Yes, it was," then oral sex is not for you. There are still so many, many loving things to do.

If you're looking to further explore oral sex, here are some tips for men:

- Sometimes a woman likes to hold back from climaxing, using oral sex as a form of foreplay, taking advantage of being wet and hot right before intercourse.
- Pauses, like silences in a conversation, are a wonderful way to build to a climax.
- Your gentle fingers can play as big a part as your tongue.
- Keep up what you're doing even as she climaxes; a woman isn't "done" with orgasm until her whole body relaxes.
- There's not one kind of orgasm; orgasms have different intensities and durations.
- Did she come? Get to know your partner's rhythms and sounds, and you'll know immediately whether she did, or not.

Some tips for women:

- Gentle massaging of the testicles and scrotum is a real man-pleaser during oral sex.
- Many men are also highly sensitive to stroking and licking of the perineum, the area between the scrotum and anus.
- If, like many men, your guy wants to hold off on climaxing until intercourse, agree that he'll give you a "Whoa!" signal when he's getting close.

- Talk beforehand about whether you will swallow his semen; if you don't want to, "finish him off" using your hands.

Advanced Oral Fun

Dessert anyone? Yes, bring food into it! Dessert is the preferred cuisine category. (Gee, I wonder why?) Favorite food items for oral sex include whipped cream, chocolate sauce, and honey.

You'll probably want to plan ahead and bring the dessert close to the bed or wherever your oral sex play is happening. Whipped cream can adorn an erect penis while the woman licks it off with long strokes of her tongue. Similarly, a man can place the cream on or around his lady's vulva, being careful not to put it directly into the vagina.

Instead of dessert, you might substitute flavored lubricants, often fruit flavored, designed specifically for use in oral sex.

DAY 16: YOUR HIDDEN PLEASURE ZONE, G WHIZ

Is there really a magic spot inside a woman's vagina that buzzes her straight into a major orgasmic convulsion, complete with ejaculation? Actually, there is in some women, and you can have some fun exploring for it.

The G-Spot

I know you've heard of it. But is its actual location a bit fuzzy to you? Well, now's the time to learn all you need to know—not because the G-spot is essential to satisfying sex (it isn't), but because it's one of those possibilities you may want to explore, to see if it fits for you and your loving partner.

To find her G-spot, the woman should first empty her bladder, because there is sometimes an urge to urinate when the G-spot is stimulated. Then she lies down with knees bent, feet flat on the bed, and a pillow under her bottom, which is a great sexual angle anyway for many women.

Partner, you gently insert a lubricated finger (nail closely trimmed, of course) into her vagina and curve it toward you, so you're feeling along the vaginal "ceiling" toward her navel. About 2 inches in, start to gently rub in a windshield wiper back-and-forth pattern or a forward "come here" stroke, whichever works better for her.

If she's one of the lucky women with a highly responsive G-spot (named for a Dr. Grafenburg about 50 years ago), the area will start to swell because there is erectile tissue behind it. As you stroke the G-spot, you can also gently stimulate her clitoris. The combination might give her an intense orgasm and maybe even female ejaculation. Although the fluid comes from her urethra, it is not urine. Its chemical makeup is similar to a man's ejaculate, just another way in which men and women have similarities. (Some researchers believe this area is a vestigial version of the prostate gland.)

If that angle doesn't work, have her roll over with a pillow beneath her stomach and try to find the spot from that angle. Remember, it's on the front, bellybutton wall of her vagina. The reason some women prefer rear-entry intercourse (doggie style) is that, for them, the penis is more likely to stimulate the G-spot from that angle. Others use woman-on-top to move so that the penis rubs the G-spot.

Although some women love to have their G-spot stimulated, others feel nothing special or may simply feel the urge to urinate. Some find it upsetting, perhaps because they think it *should* feel wonderful but doesn't. Wrong! There is no *should* to it. It just depends on how you're wired.

The important thing is not to make a big deal out of it and create performance anxiety in either of you. If it's fabulous, that's great. If it's not (and it's not for a majority of women), that's okay, too. This is a risk-free experiment, so be sure that neither of you turns it into performance anxiety.

Day 17: Sexy, Spontaneous Calls

I'm going to make the assumption that, alas, you *cannot* spend all day in bed with your sweetheart. Maybe one of you has to work late at the office, or you're away overnight on a business trip. No problem. You're going to learn how to keep the *Sizzling Sex* program going while apart from one another—in body, but not in mind.

In fact, your imaginations are going to go on overtime, as you come up with sizzling phone calls, text, or audio messages to stoke the fires until you're back in each other's arms again.

The Surprise "Come Hither" Message

Picture yourself or your honey in the middle of a business meeting when his cell phone or Blackberry vibrates in his pocket. He picks it up and puts it on his notepad just to check and see who's calling. That's when he reads your text message:

"I have a surprise for you when you get home."

Or, "I miss your body, please bring it home to me."

Or, "You can't have me for lunch, but I'd love to be your dessert tonight."

You get the idea. There's no way he's not going to spend any extra time at the office after getting one of these messages.

Phone Sex

"What are you wearing?" asks the man (in a hotel room) of his wife.

"Nothing," she answers seductively as she lies naked on their bed back home.

Men, it seems, love phone sex. A fair number of ladies also report having a good time with this form of foreplay or sex play. The main appeal of phone sex is the ability of both parties to imagine whoever and whatever they wish to be on the other end of the phone line. This is one of those situations when your mind is definitely the center of arousal.

You can do and say many different things while having phone sex with your sweetie. Once again, the purpose of this exercise is to drop something spicy into your sexual relationship. You might just save this activity to try while one of you is away from home on business; or, if you wish to try it soon, simply go to different rooms and pick up phone extensions just for the fun of experimenting.

Here are some things for the two of you to do while you're on the phone:

- One of you plays with him- or herself and narrates as you go along, as in "Now I'm squeezing my breast and moving my hand down across my belly …."

- Together you make up a story of the two of you in a wild sexual fantasy. You might want to make it edgy, something you'd never actually do.

- Both of you self-pleasure at the same time. Try simply making sounds without words.

What you're doing in each of today's exercises is staying connected in order to keep your sexual energy flowing, whether you're physically together or apart.

Be kind. It's no fair to narrate your honey through an entire encounter while he's banging out (so to speak) tomorrow's presentation on his laptop.

Day 18: Exotic Dance

Some aficionados call it *striptease,* others *pole dancing.* In public or private, exotic dance is designed to bring both dancer and watcher far out on the edge of sexual excitement. In other words, it's a tease, a turn-on.

Perhaps you've seen media reports of women buying their own dancing poles and taking secret lessons; other ladies improvising with brooms, then surprise their partners with Saturday night erotic dance performances. Today's *Sizzling Sex* activity shows you how to make erotic dance work as an aphrodisiac for you and your honey in the privacy of your own living room or bedroom.

Your assignment, if you can get comfortable with the idea (come on, give it a try), is to take turns as dancer and watcher. Yes, erotic dance is becoming all the rage for men, too … think Chippendales with your sweetie's face on that hunky dancer's body. While it may be a new idea for you men, I've heard many a woman fantasize about being a stripper, so girls, here's your chance. Let go of your inhibitions. It'll be a blast. And guys, fair's fair. You can pull off a "Full Monty" when it's your turn.

The Art of the Tease

Here's how to do an exotic dance:

1. Dress sexy, especially underneath … black or red lingerie, g-string, fishnet stockings and garters, or teddy.

2. There are no rules as to overall wardrobe … make it a baby doll dress, police uniform, nurse outfit, man's shirt, whatever

strikes your fancy. Shawls tucked into hipster panties can create a belly-dance look.

3. Wear several layers you can peel off one at a time.

4. Turn on some sexy music. Tempo should be slow and suggestive. The all-time best is "The Stripper," by Billy Rose. Download it, if you can, or buy the "Music of the Stripper" CD. Marvelous! Makes you *want* to strip!

5. With or without a pole, dance slowly in place, roll your pelvis round and round, sway your hips, and do a little hump-bump.

6. Touch and stroke your breasts and thighs while you move.

7. Toss items of clothing in your partner's direction.

8. Keep eye contact at all times.

9. No touching! But do allow your partner to put dollar bills in your panties, and encourage cheers.

10. Stretch out the finale as long as possible as you strip down to nothing … take it all off!

When one of you is finished, or buck naked, you can trade roles: play another song and do another dance.

DAY 19: THE BLIND DATE

Your date this week is a definite departure from the norm, not just for this *Sizzling Sex* program, but for however long you've been together as a couple. Tonight's date is "blind," in the sense that you'll begin the evening as a single person and end it hooked up. *But how you get there is entirely unknown.* You're not even going to leave the house together. Ideally, you should take two forms of transportation and meet at the appointed location at a selected time, but aside from this small bit of planning, everything else should be left to your spontaneous impulses.

This exercise is essentially a role-play and date night combined. You're going to enact a first meeting in a slightly risqué setting, preferably happy hour in a trendy bar or at a singles dance. The idea is to spot each other across the room and go through the paces of seduction, complete with pick-up lines, light banter, and heavy flirting. Perhaps throw in some line dancing or karaoke, all the while warming up to a finale where you'll presumably spend a very hot night together.

The key is to make it different from your usual night out. Don't go to your favorite restaurant or someplace you'll run into people you know. This is all about making the familiar unfamiliar again, adding an edge and rediscovering the chemistry that originally brought you together.

Detour: Same Ol', Same Ol'

What if you're just bored with your lovemaking? You have sex once a week or once a month, but the passion is squeezed out. Sometimes it feels like something else to tick off a to-do list.

Jason and Brenda were in this spot when they first came to me. Married for 15 years, both had jobs they liked and by now were making enough money to save and splurge occasionally. Their three kids were old enough not to require constant attention. All in all, this should have been a great time in their marriage. The problem was, their sex had become stale, even boring.

In our first session, Brenda reminisced about the early days and the rocket-surge of initial sexual attraction that made it difficult for them to keep their hands off each other. She missed those days, and so did Jason.

First of all, I let them know I completely understood. Newness is such fun, but, by definition, it can't last. That boat has sailed. However, instead of reaching back to recapture a 15-years-ago passion, now they could create something completely new.

They had married really young, with limited experience. They both thought Jason was an accomplished lover, but in truth, he'd had only a few encounters and, therefore, not many skills. Brenda was even less experienced and either didn't know or didn't feel free to ask for what she wanted. Their initial passion carried them through the first few months, but after that, they'd been Xeroxing their Xeroxes, each sexual encounter becoming a slightly paler version of the last.

My job was to help them become more intimate in all ways, not just in bed—to discover and share who they had become.

After learning something about each of them in the first session, I asked them to agree not to have sex for the next three weeks. They gave each other a knowing glance and Jason said, "So what else is new?"

I grinned and said, "I know, I get that a lot. Here's what I want you to remember. You weren't born knowing how to tie your shoes, but you learned. You may think you know everything there is about being good in bed, but you can learn more, get better, and have more fun. More important, you can get closer. Your kids will be grown and gone before you know it—now's the time to become lovers again, not just parents and spouses."

I gave them two assignments: one was conversation, the other sensual attention.

Conversation: Several times a week, find a time to just talk. What was the scariest thing from your childhood? What was the most thrilling? Who did you think you'd become as a grown-up? Who was your first crush? How could you tell when your parents were proud of you? What got you in trouble, and how did you handle it? What was the baddest thing you ever did? Was it fun?

The ground rules: Make no judgments. Don't interrupt. Take turns being the speaker and the listener. Listen with your heart as well as your ears. Feel your empathy, your bonding connection; grow a little with each story.

Sensual attention: Set the scene in a manner that's romantic to you both—candlelight, soft music, no children around. Put a bottle of lotion in warm water and take turns giving each other a hand and wrist massage. Slowly nurture every inch of skin, and lovingly explore every little bone and tendon. On another night, do the same with a foot massage.

I told Jason and Brenda that to let their relationship breathe and expand, it was important to carve out uninterrupted time together. I knew they were lonely for each other, but fortunately, neither was blaming the other. However, they did blame their busyness and considerable responsibilities. I said, "What if the lottery called and told you to come pick up your winnings? Wouldn't that be more important than doing the dishes or washing the car, or returning calls and e-mails, or whatever it is you do instead of being intimate? It's all about priorities. If you'll set aside time to watch the Super Bowl, you can make intimacy equally important. You have a choice about how you will spend your time. Choose better!"

They got it, and from that point on they went through the steps of *Sizzling Sex,* one by one. My sessions are weekly, but it didn't take them 30 weeks. In fact, within three months, they were in mature love, which they both declare beats the heck out of immature infatuation. It has power and stability, as opposed to breathless pubescent excitement and insecurity. It is based on knowledge of each other, not projected fantasies. It is also very, very sexy. They absolutely loved the *Sizzling Sex* program.

I really like those guys. They send me a Christmas card every year.

Chapter 7

FUN AND GAMES

By now you've reawakened desire, retooled your techniques, and brought the joy of sex back into your lives. In this chapter, you advance to *Sizzling Sex* grad school, bringing imagination into your sex play. From your own creative fantasies, you try on new roles and indulge impulses that have been sitting on the edge of your conscious awareness until now.

DAY 20: JOURNAL YOUR FANTASIES

Your assignment today is to come up with some sizzling fantasies. If this is new territory for you, don't worry. I'll provide some thoughts to get you started—to prime the pump, as it were.

First, though, a word on the general subject of sexual fantasies. I'd say they fall into two types: the ones you'd really like to play with in real life, and the ones you wouldn't do on a bet. You just, well, fantasize about them.

A woman might fantasize about making it with her next-door neighbor. That doesn't mean she really would. Fantasies are private thoughts to help get your libido fired up, though if you want to share them with your beloved, it can be wonderful. If you can bring your fantasies to life with your partner, you can both have a great time—maybe great sex, and at least a playful laugh.

Here are some ideas to get your dramatic juices going. Be sure to have a pen and your *Sizzling Sex* journal nearby.

The Printed Word and the Big Screen

Let's begin by taking a look at some sex-inspiring books and movies.

Who is your favorite book or screen character? In what period does s/he live? You may be the exotic and powerful Cleopatra with the Roman warrior Anthony at your feet. Or you're Anthony, and you've just returned from a conquest at sea, only to lay eyes on this exotic Egyptian queen who thrills you to the core.

What would it feel like to hold so much power over a man, or give over all your power to such a woman? As with so much that's sexual, go slowly as you let the fantasy ripen. Allow yourself to picture each enticing look, word, and touch. Will anyone else be present in this fantasy? Cleopatra's court was infamous for its orgies of aphrodisiac foods, aromas, exotic dancing, and group sex play.

Did you ever read *Lady Chatterley's Lover*? Steamy sensuality in the English countryside—a great place to start fantasizing. Imagine yourself being wildly passionate under the summer sun.

And what about the inexorable chemistry between Meryl Streep and Clint Eastwood in *The Bridges of Madison County*?

Here are some of my favorite hot movie scenes. Do you remember any of them?

Movie: *The Piano.* Mute but far-from-dumb Ada (Holly Hunter) allows herself to be the loser/winner in a psychological strip poker game with Baines (Harvey Keitel), the tattooed gone-native New Zealand settler. By the time they actually get to sex, the eroticism is all but fogging up the screen. In real life, a man could "coerce" his partner into relinquishing one garment at a time, by either reward or (pretend) punishment. This could be a very sexy game indeed.

Movie: *Out of Africa.* The eroticism is set up in the safari scene where Denys Finch-Hatton (Robert Redford) sensually shampoos Karen Blixen's hair (Meryl Streep). The actual sex scene has him saying quietly but firmly to her, "Don't move."

"But I want to move." "Don't. Move." Whew! There is tenderness there but also dominance by this super-masculine man over a strong-willed woman. A real-life couple can play that same scene. Sex can build to a powerful crescendo when it is s-l-o-w-e-d down to a torturous pace, with the partners not moving externally but pulsating together internally.

Movie: *No Way Out.* In the back seat of a limo, party-girl Susan (Sean Yonng) gleefully shucks her elegant evening gown and underwear for naval officer Tom Farrell (Kevin Costner). They are spontaneous combustion with a light-hearted undertone. The heat between them caught fire at the party, and now they're sneaking away like a couple of teenagers. It's naughty and fun and very sexy. In real life, a woman can put on sexy underwear, maybe a garter belt or thigh-high stockings, under a gorgeous gown. She and her partner can have a couple of drinks at an upscale bar or party, then park halfway home, climb in the back seat (champagne already stashed there?), and have a joyous party of their own.

Movie: *Body Heat.* Matty Walker (Kathleen Turner) smolders on the stairs as hypnotized Ned Racine (William Hurt) stares at her through the window like a deer caught in the headlights, then smashes the glass with a lawn chair and nails her on the stairs. It's animalistic, inevitable, hot hot hot. In real life, the woman becomes a seductress, using innuendo and backward glances and eventually a smoldering gaze, until her partner is caught in her tractor beam. As for the stairs, though, I recommend you substitute a more comfortable surface, okay?

Movie: *Bull Durham.* Annie Savoy (Susan Sarandon) worships baseball. Crash Davis (Kevin Costner) is a down-to-earth, honest-to-God ball player with some years on him, a no-bullshit attitude, and lots of experience. They spar from the beginning, allowing him to deliver that wonderful speech that ends, "I believe in long, slow, deep, soft, wet kisses that last three days." When they finally do have sex, he deftly unsnaps her garter with one flick, sweeps everything off the kitchen table, and away they go. Afterward they soak in a tub surrounded by candles, hot attraction plus lazy romance. In real life, I'd recommend you forgo the kitchen table, put candles all over the room, and merge the hot with the romantic. Don't forget the garter belt and stockings.

None of these may represent your ultimate fantasy of an irresistible lover. So who or what does? Imagine a mysterious man or woman who inspires you to do something risqué, someone who gets you to step outside your normal boundaries of "good" behavior. Perhaps it's a man in uniform you encounter at an airport, or an elegantly attired woman sitting alone at the bar. How does he sweep you off your feet, literally and figuratively? Now write down your fantasy of you (as you are or as you sometimes wish to be) with this person. How long does it take for the two of you to land in bed?

Once an image or some lines of dialogue come to you, write them down immediately. No censoring! This part is for no one's eyes but your own. In a few days, you'll select a fantasy from your journal to role-play with your partner. But for now, just let it rip.

On a personal note, George Clooney is always welcome in my fantasies, with that lazy, knowing grin and raised eyebrow. You're welcome to borrow him.

Fantasy Food for Thought

Did you get at least one ripe fantasy written down? Great! Save it, and savor it. Other ideas will come to you to embellish it. I also predict that as you let it roll around in your head over the next few days, you'll get more comfortable with your fantasy. Now that you've planted the seed, that internal movie might spontaneously emerge while you're waiting at a traffic light (and practicing Kegels!) or eating lunch at your desk. You're trying it on for size, visualizing in advance, like an Olympic runner before the starting shot is fired.

I know a woman who, at age 12, saw a film in which the swashbuck-ling pirate captures the lovely, fiery red-haired princess and carries her, kicking and scratching, down into his quarters. "Put on this night-gown," he growls. "I won't!" she screeches. "Put it on or I'll throw you to the crew without it!" Ooooooo. The little girl in the audience didn't know about sex yet, but even so, she got a huge tingle out of that scene.

Is that a safe fantasy to play out? It can be entirely safe, if it's your own partner as the pirate and you're *just playing.* Masterful (not cruel) seduction is still a favorite fantasy of millions of women. Author Margaret Mitchell knew exactly what she was doing in *Gone With The Wind* when she made Rhett Butler confident and master-ful.

Of course, some fantasies we would never really want to act on. By imagining a way-out scene, we have a safety valve for that deep part of us that's a bit fascinated with naughty things, or even aggres-sive or dangerous ones. Millions of people read or watch hard- or soft-core porn, or think extravagantly sexy thoughts, to get aroused. As long as it doesn't lead to behavior that disrespects, demeans, or endangers yourself or your partner, fantasize away.

People often surprise themselves with what they come up with or what they like. Early sexualizing experiences can leave their imprint for a lifetime, without your awareness. If the boy next door tied you to a tree when you were a little girl, and you squealed and squirmed to get loose but were actually getting turned on (though you didn't know it at that age), maybe getting tied up—with sensual silk scarves this time—is still a turn-on for you. It's the same with light, playful spanking, or voyeuristic peeping at each other, or sexy strutting. As long as it remains a choice for private play and doesn't become a compulsion, guess what? You're normal!

DAY 21: GIVE COMPLETELY FOR EIGHT HOURS

Sometimes my own beloved and I make a bet about something we're both so sure we're right about ("It was Julia Roberts, not Sandra Bullock!") that the loser has to be "Slave for a Day." You might want to try it; it's actually great fun and can be a turn-on, not to mention a playful "Told ya so!"

Let's say it's Saturday, you lost the bet (grrrr), and it's your turn to be Slave for a Day. For the next eight hours, you'll do whatever your partner asks of you. It might be a request to wash and massage his feet, or to walk around the house doing everything you usually do, but naked (obviously, this depends on who else is home), while he sits on the sofa watching, like an *Arabian Nights* sultan. Maybe he wants you to draw on his belly with whipped cream and then lick it off. The possibilities are endless, and fantasies can get played out with delight. Obviously, when it's his turn to be the giver, he will similarly give himself over to your fondest desire.

By now, it has probably occurred to you that it isn't necessary for a bet to be involved. You can always choose to trade Slave Days, if that's appealing and no one uses it unkindly.

As in all things, of course, you have the right to say "No" to something that really grates on you—but being a good sport can be part of the fun, especially as you fantasize about what you'll have your partner do for you when you win the next bet.

Here's the surprising part of this exercise. Though it would seem that the harder job belongs to the one serving, the opposite is often true. It can be challenging to ask for things and to receive exactly what you ask for hour after hour. For starters, you have to know what you want, then you have to get past feeling selfish or bossy when you ask for it. For many people, especially self-reliant, independent types, this is not so easy.

When you are the giver, you have to put aside any resentments you might have about who's been doing what housework or childcare. Your asking or receiving may also bring about a role exchange when it comes to who's initiating sex play. What are your boundaries? What makes you feel good in giving?

At the end of the day, share your internal experiences with each other. Of all the things your partner did or asked for, what meant the most to you? What service gave you less of a thrill than you expected?

Who knows? After you've had the chance to be giver and receiver, you may come up with new requests or ways to ask for something in sex that you've been inhibited about requesting. It doesn't have to be obvious, although the impact can be large. Just notice!

DAY 22: TAKE A BATH OR SKINNY-DIP TOGETHER

Come on, you say, what's so great about a dunk in the water? This is another seemingly obvious activity, one you don't need to be told when or how to do. But wait, when was the last time you actually got into some body of water together and simply relaxed? Trust me, when you bring the intention of creating *sexual healing* into a warm tub of water, it's a whole other experience. You might also think of today's activity as a pause, a bit of gentle, even teasing foreplay before you up the ante considerably later this week.

So in the meantime, soak. If your home bathtub is big enough for the two of you, that's fabulous—you get to stay home. But if your tub is built for one, or if there's only a shower stall, you'll need to explore other options. Maybe you have friends with a Jacuzzi you can borrow. Alternatively, many cities and towns have day spas with a heated whirlpool available. So do many gyms, YMCAs, and hotels. At some full-service spas, you can book a massage with a professional masseuse and then have access to the hot tub or pool. Check out whether you can book time or get a day pass at such a place when it's not very busy.

The idea is to connect in a womblike setting where you both can relax completely. If it's nighttime and you're alone, put lighted candles in plastic cups and let them float around you. You're aiming for the maximum possible romance without adding any pressure to perform. If you can add soap bubbles, so much the better … use a brush or washcloth and bathe each other gently from head to toe. Be playful.

If you have complete privacy, you might get frisky and not want to hold back. That's exactly what I meant when I wrote in Chapter 2 about making this program *your own.* What you do is entirely up to you. I'm only a guide, a coach.

On another personal note, my honey and I have a favorite bed-and-breakfast place in the woods, an hour's drive from home. There is a hot tub there, under the second-floor balcony to the upstairs king-size bedroom. We like to watch the sun go down in a sea of flame, or the moon rise, and then go down and get in that secluded hot tub. True, we have to swat mosquitoes, but it's worth it. I am a great believer in B&B getaways.

DAY 23: DRESS AND UNDRESS EACH OTHER

On any average day, we dress for success on the job, and then after getting home, exhausted, we put on clothes that make us feel comfortable. It can be a lifestyle of wardrobe extremes: buttoned-up shirt collars and pressed skirts during the day, baggy sweats after 5 P.M. In our seesaw lives, we rarely put on clothes with the sole objective of pleasing, even turning on, a romantic partner.

That's what this exercise is all about. On this day, you're going to go along with your honey's wishes when it comes to what you wear for your day/afternoon together or your date, and you'll do the same for her. Later, after you've gone out or spent the time relaxing at home looking like your partner's dream date, you'll have the fun taking it all off!

Now, here's the essential part of this activity. Before you get into putting on any particular dress or pants or hat, your assignment is to have your partner stand in front of you and a mirror and say what you find most *sexy* about him or her. "I love your breasts, they're so soft and beautiful." or "The curve of your waist with the backlight is fabulous." or "You look slightly dangerous in that beard, and I love it."

From this exchange, it flows naturally to have each of you, with care, pick out the other's outfit for your special outing or time together. You're charged to find the most flattering thing in your partner's closet. Or, if you like, you may buy your honey something new for the occasion.

Men, here's a word about buying your lady lingerie. When you give her a pair of skimpy black lace panties or a postage-stamp-size red silk camisole, you risk her taking your gift the wrong way. She may think you consider her usual nightclothes dowdy, or she may feel pressured to have sex immediately or more often than you currently do. If the items are too small (or large) for her, she may assume you're making a statement about her weight, when all you wanted to do was give her something pretty and feminine to say "I love you" or, better yet, "I think you're sexy." That doesn't mean you should skip lingerie as a gift. Most women do like it, especially satiny fabrics that feel good on her skin. Just be sure that you think about *her* (the colors she likes, her size) when you pick out lingerie as a gift, or pick it out together and get credit for the loving thought.

Your exercise concludes with a private *striptease,* but with a twist. For this striptease, you're going to undress each other. Before you do, think about the word *striptease* for a moment, especially the "tease" part, which connotes playful, alluring, come hither, all the qualities that make foreplay more fun when it's done slowly, teasingly. Make it a joint effort at taking things off, one at a time, enjoying each step of the dance.

Dressing Up

Just as stripping can be a turn-on, so can putting on clothes that turn your sexual foreplay into a role-play. Here's how one couple incorporated dressing up as a regular part of an unconventional intimate routine.

The husband was a highly sexed man who liked variety and fun. His wife was a former actress who loved to dress up and was crazy about costume parties. They had a costume trunk for all occasions. Among the items in this trunk: a Scarlett O'Hara garden-party hat; a wing-collared white shirt and Rhett Butler string tie; a big-sleeved pirate shirt, cummerbund, and eye patch; black lace stockings; a red garter belt; high-heeled boots; fringed shawls and silver lamé suitable for a harem; his old high school letter jacket; and a badge that could belong to a policeman, meter reader, or postal inspector.

Every now and then, one of them came home and found a stranger waiting—maybe elegant and dashing, maybe cheap and trashy, maybe exotic and seductive, maybe dangerous and authoritative. Imagine the scenes they played out! The important thing about this couple was that they both liked these games. One was not coercing the other. What fun!

DAY 24: GET CREATIVE

Okay, it's time to get out your *Sizzling Sex* journal and open it to the pages where you wrote down your private fantasies. Today you and your partner are going to act out at least one of them. Get ready. It's show time!

The two of you are alone, comfortable, and in your bedroom or another private space where there's more room to play. If you're especially well prepared, you've brought some props or costumes in to your play.

The first thing you do is tell your fantasy to your partner and listen to his in return. Often this alone will get things heated up between you. Your other purpose at this stage is to find a fantasy that appeals to both of you. If you feel uncomfortable with the fantasy, by all means, speak up and find another one that pleases you both.

While we're on the subject, you need certain ground rules about acting out sexual fantasies:

- Players must never violate the comfort zone of either partner. When in doubt, the more reserved or conservative partner's sensibilities must be honored.

- They must remain playful. It's fine to wrap a silk scarf around someone's wrists, but it's scary to be really restrained, unless it's a mutual turn-on and there is an agreed-upon *safe word* that means, "That's far enough. Back off."

Give yourself time to warm up to your character. Costumes and props help: hats, a glamorous gown for him or her, and masks are fun, too. Say the things your character would say; let go of your normal identity and simply *become her or him.* You're playing, so cut loose and enjoy yourselves. It can be fun to become an oil tycoon, or Robert Redford offering a million dollars for one night of pleasure. (And did any woman besides me think that the underlying premise of the movie *Indecent Proposal* was stupid? Turn down a million dollars to go to bed with a zillionaire played by Robert Redford? I'd do it for free!)

When you've completed your own fantasies and are wondering what else might be fun to do, you may want to read one of the many books out there containing collections of others people's fantasies. You can read them alone or aloud together. To add to the mix, here are some of my favorites, gathered from clients, friends, relatives, and my own life. But I won't tell you which is which.

- The tape recorder

   One woman left a cassette player in an easily spotted place just inside the front door, with a sign saying "Turn Me On." On it, her voice said: "I just had the greatest fantasy. You came in, got undressed, then went to the fridge and pulled out some champagne and a plate of sensual food. Then you put a couple of champagne glasses between your fingers and came upstairs. I was lying in bed reading when you walked in. There you were, in all your wonderful nakedness, bringing a party upstairs! And then you ...."

   Of course, she had planted a plate of luscious nibbles, a bottle of champagne, and two crystal champagne glasses in the refrigerator before he got home. He took it, and her, from there.

   My thought on hearing this lovely fantasy is that this couple could have gotten double the titillation (wonderful word!)

from their role-play if they had tape-recorded their lovemaking, then played it back at another time.

- Mud wrestling

Through a series of completely unforeseen events, a couple found themselves in the audience at a mud-wrestling show. They were amazed, amused, and turned on at the sight of two gorgeous bodybuilder women grappling at each other and sliding around in drilling mud, a very slippery substance used in drilling oil wells.

The wife couldn't get it out of her mind. A few days later, her husband came home to find her in a glitzy cloak over stripper-looking underwear. Like the mud wrestlers had done, she put on some sexy music and slowly stripped everything off him and herself, then led him into the bathroom, where she had put a gallon of chocolate pudding in the tub. They wrestled, slipped, laughed, licked pudding off each other, and finally showered off and went to the bedroom for their finale.

- Stereophonic massage

One woman went to massage classes and loved them. For her birthday, a friend told her to stay at home and be ready to accept a package. When the doorbell rang, she opened the door and found two lovely gentlemen. One was holding two bottles of champagne in one hand and three glasses in the other, hanging down through his fingers. The other man had a silver tray filled with strawberries.

She invited them in and they took her upstairs and gave her a marvelous stereophonic massage. These guys were massage aficionados who worked together in perfect unison like synchronized swimmers, mirroring their strokes exactly. The effect was mesmerizing, and the birthday girl had a lovely, lovely time. Afterward they drank champagne and all fed each other strawberries.

How about surprising your sweetie with a stereophonic massage? Or you both get one on your anniversary, the masseurs leave, and you make glorious love.

With any surprises at the door or elsewhere, be sure to balance the fun you imagine might happen with what you know about your sweetie's temperament. A warning may be in order, or a reassuring note from you from whoever is delivering the treat. The most important part of any fantasy role play is for each player to have the choice to "opt out" at any time!

DAY 25: BECOME EACH OTHER'S FANTASY

Until today's exercise, you've played out your role-plays strictly in your imagination or in the privacy of your own home. But now, if you're ready and willing, I'm suggesting you take your fantasies one step further, into the world. You might wear unusual (for the two of you) outfits and take on different personas. Perhaps you'll become a Southern belle, out for the night with your cowboy rancher. Might you dress up in trashy clothes and meet your "date" at a strip club? You can share an exotic, erotic show, and a safe bit of voyeurism, and you both get your sexual juices going. Ladies, you might even get a kick out of watching your man get a lap dance, then going home to try it out yourself.

DETOUR: FEAR OF FLYING

What if one of you is much more adventurous when it comes to fantasy role-playing than the other? What if your playful fantasy becomes an obsession? Laurie and David, married for three years when they came to me for sex therapy, were having severe problems because of David's insistent desire for a threesome involving another man. He didn't have a particular man in mind, but he'd recently confessed to Laurie that he'd had this fantasy many times during their relationship but had kept quiet, thinking it might upset her.

Well, he got that right! When he first broached the subject, Laurie told him calmly but firmly, "That doesn't fit for me, baby." When he continued to drop oh-come-on bombs, she got royally offended. She told him she was happy to role-play at home, but if he needed a third party to get sexually fulfilled, they needed to rethink their relationship.

Her exact words were, "This is a case of mistaken identity, David. You've mistaken me for someone who'll put up with this crap, so knock it off."

David tried to defend his fantasy by saying that what appealed to him was the idea that Laurie might submit to another man in order to please him, David, but under conditions that he could control. In other words, he wanted Laurie's unequivocal submission to him. He was clueless that such a goal just drove her further away, and faster.

Let me say here that, in my experience, people either come into a marriage already interested and probably involved in swinging, or it becomes a deal-killer to the relationship. I don't want to encourage it with people who are dubious, and I don't need to with people who are already devotees.

When I saw Laurie and David individually, it seemed to me that this was not a homosexual fantasy on his part, but it was exactly what he said: he wanted Laurie to be his creature. Of course, he'd picked the wrong girl to play that part.

She was headed for a divorce lawyer until they agreed to take a step back and reaffirm what had been working great in their relationship up to that point, including their sex, which they both said had been satisfying and actually pretty terrific. They agreed to work together for 90 days, to do the *Sizzling Sex* program from its very beginning, focusing in particular on activities designed to help couples sensually reconnect before returning to sex play. I suggested they do their activities without any notion of someone else being present, not even in David's vivid imagination.

David had to completely accept that Laurie was not available for swinging, and he had to agree not to ever bring it up again. For every couple, some activities are out of bounds because one of them says unequivocally *no*. Pornography, group sex, anal sex, humiliation, pain, water sports, whatever. If both consenting adults want it, fine—but if one is wholly opposed, it has to be off the table. Otherwise, there is subtle coercion or martyrdom, and those attitudes lead to highly dysfunctional marriages. It took a while for Laurie to feel safe again and for David to come to the adult realization that he wanted her more than his wild fantasy. In time, they were able to find ways to spice up their sex and even explore the slightly shadowy side of giving and receiving, without either feeling pushed or deprived.

Chapter 8

HOME STRETCH

At this point in your *Sizzling Sex* program, I hope you and your sweetheart are feeling much closer than before you started. It's not just because you're having sex again, although that's a lovely thing. It's also because you've restored intimacy between the two of you. No longer ships passing in the night, you're not simply running a household or raising kids together anymore. You've reconnected at the heart level, and that makes *everything* better.

Chances are, you're also spending more of your time, together and apart, *thinking* about sex. This phenomenon of having "sex on the mind" can affect all areas of your life. Not only have you freed up your passions in the bedroom, but you get the bonus benefit of having more passion everywhere. Doing everyday chores, you may notice you feel more alive, your body practically buzzing with energy. In these final five days of our program, I help you seal the deal by further cultivating this greater capacity for pleasure, in and out of the bedroom. You'll also be planning your personal graduation ceremony in the form of a sizzling dream date.

DAY 26: PUSH THE BOUNDARIES

Some of your earliest sexual experiences was the self-comforting you gave yourself as a baby or toddler. You may not even have known the word for what you were doing as you continued to sexually stimulate yourself throughout childhood and your early teen years. Today, in one of our regular exercises focused on self-preparation for better lovemaking, I'll be your guide for some enhanced techniques for self-pleasuring, a word I prefer to masturbation.

Unfortunately, a lot of people see self-pleasuring either as obscene or as something people do only if they don't have a sexual partner. Actually, it can be like spring training: the more you do it, the better you get at knowing when and how to reach your goal. Not only do you get personal gratification, but you also learn the fine points of your own pleasure zones, so you know what to ask for with your partner or how to move to get your best gratification.

Your climax isn't an experience someone gives you, regardless of what pop culture would have you believe. It arises from within you. And the more familiar you are with how to release it, the more you will enjoy all aspects of sex.

The Basics of Self-Pleasuring

Self-pleasuring is, by definition, a gift you give yourself. Although it can indeed be a prelude to sex with your partner, it's also a way you can nurture yourself when you're alone. Does that critic in your head call it selfish? Well, only if a warm bubble bath or massage is considered selfish, and in my book (as it were), these are simply ways you relax and take care of yourself.

- A man usually enjoys a slow up-and-down sliding motion, gradually increasing in pace. He can show his partner just how he likes it, and when she combines it with gentle kissing or sucking of the penis, it's a sure-fire way to heat him up to the broiling stage. Of course, there will be times when he just wants to pleasure himself, privately or with her as a fascinated audience.

- Many women prefer a light, teasing touch directly on their clitoris. Others prefer a cupped hand on their whole genital area, with some pressure in a round-and-round or up-and-down motion. Still others like the penetration of a damp finger slowly stroked in and out of the vagina, pulled forward to stimulate the clitoris, then inserted fully again.

Get to know your own arousal signals. Learn when you intuitively want the motions faster or slower, and when you prefer firmer or lighter stroking. It's also worth noting what's going on (What time of the day is it? Are you stressed or relaxed?) when the urge for self-pleasure comes to you. Are you more of a morning or evening person? By becoming aware of your cycles of heightened arousal, you'll recognize and take advantage of those times when you're in the mood to initiate sex or take steps to make it at least an option for you and your partner.

The Toy Shop

Toys can quicken and intensify arousal and add sexual stimulation and pleasure when you're alone. They are also handy when used with your partner before or during sexual intercourse.

Your handiest attachment, literally, is at the end of your wrist. However, some women need the more intense stimulation provided by a vibrator.

Sometimes called "personal massagers," vibrators are the primary sex toy used and enjoyed by women. They can be battery operated or electric powered, and most have variable speeds. The battery-driven ones are usually penis-shaped plastic shafts, often sheathed in rubber to look lifelike. Although these toys resemble an erect penis, many women do not insert them, but rather use them to directly or indirectly stimulate the clitoris. Women who do want to insert them may choose a model that has a second, smaller shaft to buzz the clitoris while the major part of the vibrator is inside.

The electric vibrators really do resemble massagers, are actually used as both, and often have a knob or other attachment to conduct vibrations to your pubic bone, vulval area, and clitoris. They are often quieter than their battery cousins and have the advantage of never running out of power. It can be very frustrating to be using a battery-driven vibrator and have the battery give out just as you're close to climax.

It's a trade-off, really. An AC massager can get hot after a prolonged self-pleasuring session and, obviously, requires an electric outlet. The battery-operated vibrator requires a fully charged battery (and maybe a couple of spares on the nightstand) and doesn't last forever.

A favorite vibrator can be a good friend at times when, as Charlotte said in the TV series *Sex and the City,* a certain part of your anatomy has been feeling depressed.

Men, bless their hearts, are much less complicated in the arousal and climax department. The only equipment they usually need for self-pleasuring is their own experienced hand. As for male sex toys, the most popular is a circle of rubber or steel that goes on the base of the penis to help it become erect and stay that way. A well-placed ring enhances his sensations during self-pleasuring or intercourse. A word of warning: be sure to get a quick-release model!

So experiment! Find what works for you to reach sexual arousal and/or gratification, whether it is your hand, a vibrator, or any other stimulation that you get for yourself.

These playthings are available at your local condom store, where you can see them up close. However, many people prefer to shop online. (See Appendix B for some sources.) Rule of thumb: up to a point, the more they cost, the better they are. A $10 vibrator can let you down at a crucial moment, but a $40 one can brighten your life for years. Be aware that each woman has her own perfect vibration, so if the first one doesn't buzz you to a fabulous orgasm, try another before you give up. And always choose one with variable speed.

Erotic Media

Many men like to get aroused with the visual aid of pictures or movies. Women, on the other hand, often prefer reading an erotic or soft-porn story. Many couples like to watch soft-core porn DVDs at home before lovemaking. You'll want to do some research to avoid the kind you find offensive. The Internet is a great place to find other people's reviews of a particular book or DVD. Just go to a search engine and enter the title and the word "review."

DAY 27: PLAN YOUR DREAM DATE

Anticipation can give us *nearly* as much pleasure as any *main event* in our sex lives. Today's activity is centered on planning your upcoming *Sizzling Sex* graduation. You'll be celebrating this important milestone with a dream date of your own mutual design.

The lovely thing about this collaboration is that it can get to be a habit. Even after many years together, about every three months, one of you might say, "Hey, baby, isn't it about time for a B&B weekend?" A bed and breakfast getaway can recharge your emotional, physical, spiritual, and sexual energies.

Here are some tips for planning your dream date:

* Have you noticed how sometimes the one who doesn't plan an event seems less invested in its outcome? To make sure you're equally on board, plan your *Sizzling Sex* graduation date *together:* where, what, when, and how much to spend.

Make lists of options, discuss, and don't rush the decision. Savor the anticipation!

♦ Secure a babysitter well in advance—Grandma, friends, a neighbor's kid, or a reliable sitter service. If you've never used a babysitter, now would be a great time to start.

♦ Don't go out on your date straight from work or athletics. Take time to bathe, relax, and decompress from the earlier part of the day.

♦ Make it truly special. Dress up.

♦ If you go out to eat, make sure it's a restaurant where you can actually hear each other talk and where you know the food is good, the service is superior, and the ambience is romantic.

♦ You might want to include some cheek-to-cheek dancing. It's a perfect way to make the evening festive and enjoy a bit of psychological foreplay on the dance floor.

♦ If the budget allows, book a hotel room in the your city or a B&B in a nearby town, whatever spells r-o-m-a-n-c-e to you.

♦ A special note to you outdoorsy types: if you'd rather celebrate al fresco, go camping where you can make love under the stars. Forget the dressing up part. Just bring good pillows and mosquito repellent, excellent finger food, and maybe a boom box with your favorite music.

DAY 28: TEASE EACH OTHER WITH TOUCH

This exercise allows you to practice what I hope becomes a permanent state of your (renewed) relationship: playful, affectionate touch. I'm encouraging you to make it important and touch each other very consciously for one entire day or weekend, taking every opportunity to physically connect with each other. Just remember, this is nondemand touching—touching for its own sake, with no goal in mind. Yet.

How to Approach It

Touching, that's it? That's easy, you may say. Well, it is and it isn't. After the first few years of a love relationship, many couples unconsciously settle into a hands-off habit, even in the privacy of their own home. Many men reserve a sensual caress of a breast or behind just for when they want to signal an interest in sex. Many women, feeling amorous but not erotic, stop themselves from a cuddle or hug because they don't want to send a false signal. Both may be starved for affection simply because they've reserved caresses, hugs, and kisses for preambles to sex.

If you see yourselves in that picture, it's time to make a new one. On a day or weekend the two of you select, you're going to go to the opposite extreme and touch each other often and tenderly. That means keeping eye contact and placing a hand on your partner's forearm when she talks. It means grazing thighs on purpose when you sit on the sofa, and much, much more.

Remember All Those Sensitive Zones

Don't forget the body parts we don't think of as erogenous but are actually among the most sensitive to touch. The scalp, earlobes, and, oh, those feet! If your honey is hunched over the computer paying bills online, pause and massage his neck and shoulders. If the two of you are out shopping or getting the car washed, don't just stand there watching the rollers soap up and rinse off your car. Encircle her waist from behind and kiss her neck. It will all come back to you as soon as you take off the invisible restraints you've put on the physical part of your relationship outside of the bedroom.

Did you get taught that PDA (public displays of affection) are not socially acceptable? Then rethink that notion. We're not talking here about groping each other on a quilt in the park (though it's a lovely thought)—just a kiss, a nuzzle, a bit of hand-holding. If the bluenoses around you sniff in disapproval, just pity them.

What if it feels awkward or unnatural after so long? Just do it! The old saying "Act as if ..." comes in handy here. If you don't have the confidence to do or say something because you're out of practice, just go ahead and do it anyway. Chances are, the reaction will be positive, too.

DAY 29: ROMANCE EACH OTHER WITH "30 THINGS I LOVE ABOUT YOU"

The fastest cure for relationship boredom is *romance*—focused attention with affection. Men and women both secretly want to be appreciated and celebrated. The point of this exercise is for you both to reclaim romance and make it your own.

Really, What Is Romance?

In medieval times, a love of God and of the beloved person meshed in the chivalric tradition of romantic poetry. At its essence, these songs and words were an expression of adoration for the beloved, with the commitment that a knight (in shining armor or otherwise attired) would be willing to lay down his life for the lady he adored.

These declarations of love and signs of adoration were sung or spoken, nonmaterial gifts of feeling and spirit. That is exactly what you're going for in this exercise. Even though we've come a long way from such traditions, your observance of a wedding anniversary and

Valentine's Day arise from that same deep desire to deeply love and be loved in return. Today's exercise will help get your own romantic juices going.

How to Create Your List

Look into your heart and come up with a list of 30 things you love about your partner. You can write your items on a special card, or type it and print the page, then put it in a scented envelope. You might also hand it to your beloved with a beautiful rose. Make it simple but special.

Here are some of the loving things I've heard spouses say to each other while doing this exercise. Keep in mind that each sentence starts with the words "One of the things I love about you is" ...."

- The loudest, merriest laugh of anyone I know
- The twinkle in your eyes when you think I look sexy
- The way you spoon with me at night
- Your singing voice, especially in church
- Your smart taste in clothes
- Your homemade pasta and meatballs
- The way you keep your eyes open when we make love
- The way you always meld with me when I come

And so on. Maybe one of these also applies to your partner. Pick any that ring true and add others that are unique to you and your sweetie. Every relationship is different, and there's a reason why the two of you work as a couple. Dig down and figure out 30 reasons why you love this man or woman. Tap into the deep devotion that's within you but that perhaps you've never given voice to.

DAY 30: CELEBRATE WITH YOUR DREAM DATE

The stars are aligned, and so are you and your beloved, ready to become *Sizzling Sex* grads by putting together everything you've learned in one dazzling dream date.

By now you've finalized your choice of what, where, and when to have this date. Take some time early in the day to iron out the details. If you're leaving town, make sure you've got a full gas tank and maps. Leave a note with your phone number for the babysitter, telling her to call only if she deems it absolutely necessary. This is your time for each other!

After you have dined, danced, romanced, champagned, and are finally in the bedroom, here are some suggestions for a memorable graduation night. Think of it as a menu from which to choose for this date and many nights to come.

- Kiss each other's bodies all over. Remember neck, earlobes, nipples, ankles, arch of the foot, back of the knee, forehead, and cheeks—all four cheeks.

- Pleasure each other with oral sex to the extent that feels right. Push your comfort level a little, but not to the turn-off point.

- Start rocking your pelvises, gently curving them up and back, while doing your Kegel exercises.

- Sir, put your lady on a pillow and begin exploring for her G-spot. Her job is to give you feedback, tell you what feels good and what doesn't, ask for you to go slower, faster, softer, firmer, or never mind.

- Stroke each other's penis and vulva until you are both very aroused.

- Make lovemaking the finale of your Day 30 dream date night. Remember, lovemaking starts with sensual touch of all kinds. Stoke arousal to an insistent pitch before intercourse begins. See how long you can prolong the pleasure to your ultimate mutual satisfaction.

- Experiment with new positions and locations if you want to, but the main goal is connection, not novelty. For a while, there is almost no separation between the two of you. Feel that soul connection.

- Linger awhile, holding each other. Enjoy the afterglow.

Congratulations on journeying through these 30 days of sizzling sex activities with an open mind and heart. Wherever you are physically on this graduation night, the two of you have gone, emotionally and sexually, to another planet.

Chapter 9

HOW TO KEEP IT SIZZLING

In this final chapter, I touch on the issues that typically get in the way of *Sizzling Sex* and how to get past them. Then I offer some of my favorite tips for keeping the sizzle in your relationship forever.

OVERCOMING ROADBLOCKS

To begin with, if you and your partner encounter one of these roadblocks, know that you're not alone. Sometimes just knowing that, and being willing to take a step back and figure out what's really going on, will help you find a way to work through the issue on your own.

In my 30 years as a sex therapist, I've found that many of the roadblocks to sizzling sex concern the always-shifting ground of *who wants sex, who doesn't, and what to do until you both get on the same page.* There are different reasons for your respective libidos at different times, some emotional, others physical. This chapter covers some basic information that will help you understand what's going on in your relationship and how to deal with it.

Libido: His, Hers, and Ours

Libido is another word for sex drive or urge. As you might suspect, this is not an on/off situation. You'll encounter gray areas, times when you're sort of ready for sex but easily distracted from it. Plenty of times also will arise when one of you is ready and the other isn't, for any number of reasons.

There's still a crazy myth out there that we should always be 100 percent rarin' to go at *all times.* Therefore, this myth goes, if your partner *is* ready and you *aren't,* there's something wrong with you *or* him *or* the relationship. To dispel this myth, I like to compare sexual appetite to the appetite for food. Sometimes you're super hungry, eager for the pleasure of a good meal. A friend asks you to go to lunch, and your reaction is, "You bet, I'm starving. Let's go right now!"

Other times you might say, "I'm not very hungry, but I'll come along and keep you company. Maybe I'll get interested after we get there." Then there are times when your answer is, "I couldn't look at food right now. Thanks anyway." Or maybe, "I've got a lot on my mind right now, and I need to stay with it. Thanks anyway."

Would your friend take any of this personally? Of course not. You're talking about yourself, not your buddy. Besides, your friend isn't always hungry, either. That same eagerness, neutrality, or absence of appetite happens in sex—all the time! It's part of the cycle of life.

Isn't it amazing, though, how defensive we can get about another person's current appetite for sex? We start telling ourselves scary stories that it's about *us,* about our own lack of appeal. Sure, occasionally it might be, but I hope by this point in the *Sizzling Sex* program, both of you are sending and receiving clear I-messages ... how *you* feel, not what your partner is "making" you feel. When you own your own feelings, you're one step closer to clear communication.

When You're Just Not Hungry

I'll explore this appetite analogy further. Let's say you are urgently turned on; for whatever reason, you crave sex right now, the same way you replied, "Yes, let's go!" to your friend's lunch invitation. Maybe it's the newness of love, or honeymoon excitement, or make-up sex, or an erotic dream. Perhaps you just closed an important deal, or got an appreciative glance from someone at the gym, and you're feeling mighty fine and want to share your happiness with your beloved.

At another time, you're less than enthusiastic but feeling companion-able, the way you went along to lunch with your friend in hopes that your appetite might kick in when you got to the restaurant. Maybe you're a little tired, a bit distracted, but you know from experience that once you get to the bed and the caressing, you'll start to have a good time. Your beloved gets things started, and before you know it, you're glad you said "Yes."

However, sometimes your sexual appetite is nowhere to be found. Your honey is hot to trot, but you definitely are not. Maybe it's hor-mones, stress, worry, or fatigue. You may even be pissed off at him and currently see him as *the enemy.* (That happens occasionally to everybody.) For whatever reason, you actively *do not want* to make love right now.

Sometimes your desire for sex disappears *after* you've started making love. That's because these same three scenarios—starving, agreeable but not enthusiastic, or no way—can still happen. Maybe you were totally with the program until the baby cried, and then the erotic spell was broken for you. Or perhaps one of you is taking a longer time to climax and the other's attention is starting to wander. These things happen, and it's nobody's "fault." Sex is sometimes ho-hum or boring—it just doesn't catch fire. Not every single encounter moves the earth.

You've been there. One minute you are happily rock-and-rolling with your lover, and then you're gone. It's about you, not your partner, and you need to simply tell your truth. "Honey, right now my mind is on the exam. Let's wait till tomorrow night." "Sorry, I can't concentrate with Uncle Harry in the guest room. How about this weekend, after they leave?" "Honey, I need more lubrication. That medicine is giving me dry mouth, and I mean everywhere."

Maybe you grew up in a stoic household where people were supposed to grin and bear it. No pain, no gain. But if you stonewall how you're feeling or what you want, your beloved may start up with those insecurities we're all vulnerable to because of the crazy myth I started this section with, the one that goes … "What am I doing wrong? Why is my partner rejecting me?"

Sometimes one partner's disinterest in sex *is* rejection or passive-aggressive payback, but not often. There's usually a very good reason why you aren't dancing to exactly the same rhythm as your lover. It's like the lunch invitation. Hungry? Not hungry? Open to the idea? Not right now? Maybe later? If I eat at your house and ask you to pass the salt, that's not a comment about how you grilled the steak. It's just that I'd like to have more salt. It's that simple. Well, it's that simple if the topic is steak. Where human beings are concerned, of course, nothing is ever really simple.

There may be a disparity in your individual sex drives. Some people just need a few days to recharge their sexual batteries between love-making times. If you want it daily and your partner wants it once a week, surely you can work out a compromise so you don't feel abandoned and your partner doesn't feel coerced. Beware the potential power struggle, though. When there is a real, ongoing difference in libido, it's important to keep affection alive and well.

Here's the scenario to avoid. Let's say the woman is the one with the less insistent libido. Even though she hasn't built up a full sexual charge since the last lovemaking, she loves her honey and they have an extravagantly sensual Friday night, satisfying to both. The next morning he says, "So how about that again tonight? No? How about tomorrow morning? Sheesh, how long to I have to wait *this* time?"

She feels pressured and inadequate. He feels rejected and angry because sex is the only way he feels legitimately loved. He implies that she's not much of a woman, and she implies that he's an insensitive jerk.

It's time for an empathy trip for both of them. (And by the way, this little drama often has the same script but with swapped roles.)

Before you interpret your partner's lack of enthusiasm as being a message about you, consider these questions. Is this person exhausted from trying to do too many things in too little time? In mourning from a loss? Just getting over a physical problem, or childbirth? Worried about a business deal, or the overhead, or the possible loss of a job?

If all else fails, it's absolutely time for some couple's counseling or coaching, because having a objective third party can do wonders to ease, translate, educate, understand, and reassure.

THE THREE D'S: DISTRACTION, DISSATISFACTION, AND DYSFUNCTION

When something goes wrong sexually, all kinds of circumstances can interfere with the natural expression of intimacy, sexual response and function, and sensual pleasure. Usually the cause is one of the Three D's: distraction, dissatisfaction, and/or dysfunction. Let's look at these roadblocks—and, remember, there's often some overlap among them.

Distraction

Why might you become distracted from lovemaking? Perhaps your mind chatters with business or child concerns, or financial problems. Those concerns reflect real life, but this is not a good time to deal with them. Besides, I highly doubt that you'll find a solution to any such problem while your attention is half on sex, and you're already feeling guilty about not being fully present with your partner. At these times, remember this: *your mind is not always your friend.* Try to tell your mind gently (or not so gently), "We can get back to that later!"

- Unfinished business from the past

  You might have unresolved feelings from a past relationship, and you find another's face appearing now where it doesn't belong. Just trying to stay in the present can take up so much of your mental and emotional energy that you're drained and have no libido left.

  You can go two ways here. Either make the decision to put the past in the past, or level with your beloved about your feelings of insecurity. As always, use the I-message: "Honey, I had a bad dream last night where I felt trapped, the way I did with (fill in the blank). Let's have an extra cuddle or plan a date tonight. Just know that if I seem distracted, it's not about you or us. It's just old ghosts, and I'm exorcising them as fast as I can."

- Body image

  One of you might not be available for sex these days because of a poor body image, another form of distraction. If so, it's time to work on your SF—your strut factor. Do what it takes to get that "Yeah!" about yourself. Go buy a sexy outfit … not one that your partner thinks is sexy, but one that makes *you* feel sexy or elegant. A man might get silk pajamas or very short shorts. A woman might get a silk sheath that falls gracefully from spaghetti straps down to her instep. Don't succumb to a stereotype. If the black garter belt and fishnet stockings don't increase your own personal strut factor, pass them up for something that does.

Get back in touch with your body, using some of the sensual exercises from earlier in the program, like long luxurious baths and all-over lotion. Get a massage and a facial, and really feel your skin soak up that nurturing attention.

Dance! Make a tape or CD of your favorite upbeat, feel-good songs and dance with yourself, by yourself, moving any way that feels right. Sway, circle, stretch your head upward and your arms out as you dance all around the house. Do some pelvic rolls, circling first clockwise, then counterclockwise. If you have a big exercise ball, sit on it and bounce; sashay left and right like a flirty kid.

Stride! Experiment with walking in longer strides, shoulders back and down, chest up, neck long. Let your arms swing naturally. You'll feel more alive with each step.

Let your partner tell you with hands-on loving how dear your body is. The best antidote to shutting down is to simply choose to open up. It really is a choice, you know.

Dissatisfaction

What if you're just bored or find lovemaking with your partner unfulfilling? For one thing, remember that the rocket-surge of initial sexual attraction is powered by newness. However, skill/attention/recommitment/communication can create something just as satisfying. Maybe you married really young, were relatively (or totally) inexperienced, and need some skills and techniques to liven things up. Even if you thought you were quite the stud or sex queen when you met, it's possible that you hadn't really had five years of experience. Maybe you'd just had one year of experience five times.

Maybe you and your partner aren't a good emotional fit at this moment. Many issues that can get in the way:

- Your partner doesn't know what you really want, and vice versa.
- Somebody else's face (a previous lover) keeps getting in the way.
- You're keeping score about who initiates lovemaking more often.
- You're bored, stale, unromantic, distant.
- You feel overworked and underappreciated.
- You're bogged down in day-to-day junk.
- You forget that there are so many ways to make love besides intercourse.

What can you do about any of these problems of dissatisfaction?

- *Learn.* Perhaps you just need some lovemaking education they didn't teach in school (or the locker room or slumber party). How do you get some remedial education in the lovemaking arts? Read books, watch erotic films, do a little research on how to be a better lover. There are scads of books on the subject, some of them quite good (see my recommended reading list in Appendix B). Get to a bookstore and start looking them over, and then buy a couple that appeal to you. You may think you know everything there is about being good in bed, but I'll bet you can learn more, get better, and have more fun.

- *Talk.* Talk it out! Ask respectfully but directly for what you want. Your partner is not a mind reader. Of course, it could be that one or both of you is hanging on to old resentments. It's also possible that you had an unpleasant experience long ago. If so, it may be time for sex or relationship coaching, or psychotherapy.

Dysfunction

One partner's sexual dysfunction can discourage both people, if they let it. Be aware, however, that there is a fix for almost every dysfunction. Let's take some common ones, examples from couples I have helped to work through them.

Erectile Difficulties

Also know as ED—erectile dysfunction, this is a chronic inability to achieve or maintain an erection. I emphasize *chronic* because almost all men have had a fleeting experience with it. If a guy is fairly knowledgeable, he can stay cool and realize it was just because he was distracted, fatigued, under the influence of alcohol, coming down with the flu, etc.

Too often, though, he tells himself with horror, "I'm impotent!" and that becomes a self-fulfilling prophecy. The next time he comes to bed, he obsesses to himself, "Please, please let me get a hard-on! Please!" Since no one can will an erection, his anxiety creates the same outcome, and now he is in real trouble with performance anxiety.

Maybe he gets a prescription from his doctor for Viagra, Cialis, or Levitra, and when he gets his confidence back, he doesn't need it anymore. Better yet, a few sessions of sex therapy can often overcome performance anxiety. On the other hand, there can be other causes of ED. Some medications, notably some that combat hypertension, can have ED as a side effect. Some disease states can also cause it: nerve damage from diabetes, multiple sclerosis, chronic alcoholism, depression, and vascular disease.

Hormones play an important part in sexual functioning, of course. One of the first things a man should do is have a complete physical, including an assessment of his testosterone level. Sometimes making healthy lifestyle changes can be the answer: stop smoking, get to the gym, lose weight, and cut back on alcohol.

A further word about smoking: the more you smoke, the higher your chance of impotence. Smoking affects blood flow, and blood flow to the penis is what creates an erection. One study found that men who currently and formerly smoked were 30 percent more likely to experience ED than nonsmokers. Now that's a heavy incentive to kick the habit!

What about age? Aren't older guys just less virile than young men? It depends on your definition of *virile*. Teenagers do get erections very easily, but they don't usually make very good lovers because not only are they unskilled, but they are hair-triggered. An older man takes longer to get hard than a young man, but he can last longer. The same love play that gets him erect can get her highly aroused, and if he is at all sophisticated in the art of love, he can play his lady like a Stradivarius violin.

One of my favorite clients of all time was a guy I'll call Harry. He'd been a jock in college and had a high strut factor, but without arrogance. He wasn't a pain-in-the-neck narcissist, just a fellow with healthy self-esteem, a darling wife, and a good career.

Then Harry ran into some serious financial problems. He made some unwise decisions and got taken to the cleaners by unscrupulous partners. He was anxious about money, embarrassed by his own gullibility, and worried about possible bankruptcy. Harry was having a hard time, but his penis wasn't.

I told him this story. I once had a woman client (let's call her Sue) who found herself middle-aged and unexpectedly back in the single world. She began to date an old friend (we'll call him Stan) who had also lost a spouse, and as their friendship deepened, they decided to take it to a sexual level.

As they stood beside the bed, kissing and caressing, Stan said, "Now, there's something you should know. Ol' Pete is a little shy, but when he gets to know you, he'll come to the party." Sue laughed long and loud, relieved to know she wasn't the only nervous person in the room. She said, "Well, you tell Pete that we know lots of ways to enjoy each other whether he shows up or not." And, of course, as their relationship progressed and Stan relaxed into the pleasure of her body and his own, Ol' Pete showed up.

My new client Harry roared with laughter when I told him this story. He then went home to his own lovely wife and told the story to her, and from then on they were both okay. Harry got his strut factor back.

Indeed, the best antidote for erectile dysfunction is simply to relax. Breathe deeply. Pay attention to all the pleasure your whole body is receiving. Tell Ol' Pete he can come to the party when he's ready, and if he's on "temporary leave of absence," just have fun without him. Once he's over his stage fright, he'll probably reappear and act just as cocky as ever.

However, if Ol' Pete doesn't return after a couple of weeks, make an appointment for a physical exam, including checking your testosterone level. Impotence might be a signal of a more serious medical condition.

Diminished Libido

As I have said, this is a lack of sex drive or a disinterest in sex, and it's the most common presenting problem that sex therapists see today. More often it's the woman who has a missing or low libido, although it happens to men, too.

The causes can be simple or complex, and usually several affect her at the same time. The most prevalent cause is stress, brought on by hurry, scurry, worry, deadlines, to-do lists, too much to accomplish in too little time, not enough down time for herself, a desire to be all things to all people, inability to say no, too many roles, too little sleep. While you may need to seek professional treatment, you might first find quick solutions in these suggestions. Most important, put your worry/scurry/hurry and to-do list on hold for right now. As the poster from the 1960s said, "Lose your mind and gain your senses."

In other cases, however, a physical problem needs to be addressed. For example, testosterone is essential in libido, and an insufficiency can shoot down your sex drive. By all means, get a complete workup with your gynecologist. If your doctor prescribes testosterone cream, you might be amazed at the improvement in your body and attitude.

A client of mine I'll call Sally had been to many gynecologists in despair over her absence of libido, which used to be strong and wonderful. By the time she found me, she had almost given up hope, and so had her husband, who made it clear that although he loved her dearly, to him, a happy marriage had to include a sex life. She had a double whammy: she had lost connection with her sexuality and now faced the possibility of losing her marriage.

I referred her to a gynecologist, a close colleague of mine, who discovered that she was deeply androgen-deficient and, in fact, was a textbook case of hypoactive sexual desire disorder. Symptoms can include a diminished sense of well-being, persistent and unexplained fatigue, and decreased libido, sexual receptivity, and pleasure. He prescribed a testosterone cream, made at a compounding pharmacy to his specifications. (These creams can be applied directly to the clitoris or can be simply stroked onto the arm. Some are created for insertion into the vagina.

Within a very short time, Sally had her beloved sex drive back. She and Sam went from having sex once every couple of months to having sex several enthusiastic times a week. As an added bonus, she lost eighteen pounds and gained far more energy. Her nails and hair started to grow, and her self-esteem also shot up over the moon.

The Post-Partum Timeout

Your sleep is chronically interrupted by feeding and changing your new wiggler, you haven't graduated from your maternity pants despite having given birth two months ago, and you still wince every time you even think of that episiotomy. Is it really surprising that your libido can best be described as lackluster?

Of course not. Most new mothers will, for a time, have no interest in sex. Not only are they hormonally challenged, but they're exhausted.

Even once she heals physically, a new mom can drag emotionally. She may be self-conscious about her postpartum body and feel anything but sexy. She may have tender breasts, making romantic contact uncomfortable. She may even worry about getting pregnant again.

As if that's not enough, it's not uncommon for a woman's romantic feelings for her partner to be eclipsed by her focus on her baby. She's having an intense affair with the little one. A wise, grown-up husband will understand, support her, and just wait it out. By the time the baby's walking, his sex partner will probably be back.

Depression and Decreased Libido

One symptom of depression is loss of libido. If you think you are depressed, make an appointment with a psychiatrist. Why? A psychiatrist is a medical doctor who is an expert in prescribing and monitoring psychotropic meds. Your family doctor or gynecologist is also a physician, but the psychiatrist is the real expert in this area.

Depression is not a failure of character; it's a chemical imbalance in the brain. Your neurotransmitters, the chemical messengers that move electrical impulses between neurons, can get out of balance. Certain medications can put them back into balance. Trying to get over depression—not temporary sadness, but real depression—without meds is like swimming with an anvil tied around your ankle.

Some antidepressive meds can interfere with libido. How's that for a Catch-22? Your sex drive is down because you're depressed, but the meds deplete your sex drive. Don't despair; your doctor can usually adjust your medications till you're in the win/win stage.

Whether you're depressed or not, make a commitment to take better care of yourself: better nutrition, more alone time or with-your-buddies time, naps, short vacations, mosey mode. All these can help.

A Word About Chemical Interactions

If you're taking any medications, ask your doctor whether they could be affecting your libido. Certain meds for high blood pressure or high cholesterol, and some antidepressants (not all) can definitely interfere with sexual desire or functioning.

And then there are recreational drugs, most commonly alcohol and nicotine. Alcohol can turn you on initially and then depress all your systems, including sexual ones.

Painful Intercourse

This is a problem with many of my women clients. It can be caused by vaginal dryness, inadequate arousal, tightness of the vaginal opening, low-grade infection, a disparity in size of penis and vagina, infrequency of intercourse, hormonal changes, or conditions such as vaginismus (involuntary tightening of the vagina) or vulvar vestibulitis (chronic irritation of vaginal tissues), a condition that creates chronic irritation and pain in vaginal tissues.

Inadequate lubrication, in my clinical experience, is the leading cause of painful intercourse. Regardless of its cause, which a doctor needs to determine and treat, the immediate solution is better lubrication! That can be naturally produced by arousal or applied with personal lubricants available at any drug store. It also requires a tender lover, at least at the beginning of a lovemaking session.

Once the vagina gets lubricated, more vigorous action can be fun for both, but you must be a little patient and go s-l-o-w when starting out. We all tense up when we anticipate pain, and starting out slowly gives the woman's body a chance to relax. It also sets the tone of luxurious, sensual sex, the very opposite of "wham-bam-thank-ya-ma'am."

Sometimes dyspareunia is chronic and difficult to overcome, particularly when it, too, has become a self-fulfilling prophecy. Often, however, your pain is the result of dryness, tightness, sensitivity, or fear of pain based on past experience. Using a good lubricant made for women can alleviate dryness and tightness. I advise against KY jelly, as your momma may have suggested, because it is sticky and works against the silky lubrication you want. However, the KY people now make good personal lubricants, as do the manufacturers of many other "feminine products."

I often recommend AstroGlide. Years ago, the only places in my conservative city that carried it were adult bookstores. I explained to a woman client that it was a little uncomfortable to go there, but she should just walk in confidently and ask the check-out clerk for it. She came back the next session and told me, with a laugh, "Roz! They sell it at Target!" Time had moved on and hadn't updated me. Now, of course, there are condom shops in many shopping centers and women's personal lubricant sold at every drug store.

One of my women clients recently discovered Carrageenen, which advertises as "most like me." She says that, for her, that's true. I love it when my clients educate me.

In my opinion, there is an optimal way to use lubricant. Instead of inserting it into your vagina, I recommend that your partner apply it to his erect penis and then nestle its head at the opening of your vagina: just the head, or maybe an inch more, until you say, "Stop." Now just hold each other and continue stroking and kissing, until your vagina begins to relax, no longer anxious that it's going to be rammed. Little by little, the penis will slide inside, but *no pushing!*

Once his penis is inside you, just soak for a while, without moving. You can tighten and release your vagina, squeezing the penis with your Kegel contractions, but no thrusting friction yet. Then, when you start to feel safer, he can begin s-l-o-w movement. If you feel squeaky anywhere inside your vagina, ask him to slowly withdraw his penis and put some more lubrication on it. Eventually you will start feeling creamy inside, as your own lubrication joins the show.

S-l-o-w is the order of the day. After this kind of experiment, your vagina may well open more easily in the future. However, some women just have tight vaginas, no matter how many children they've borne. If you're one of them, you may need to start slowly every time.

It's worth it, not only to you, but to your partner. He doesn't want to hurt you! He also has a vested interest in your looking forward to sex, not being afraid of it.

If this technique, practiced several times over a two-week period, doesn't alleviate your pain, it's definitely time to get checked out by your gynecologist. You'll not only want your hormones evaluated, but you'll also want your doctor to rule out infections or a localized sensitivity.

Also, if self-examination with a mirror and a flashlight indicates redness or other signs of irritation, don't try intercourse until you've seen your doctor.

Vulvar Vestibulutis (VV)

VV is much more common that most people realize. A few years ago, I wrote to about 500 gynecologists in my area to educate them about VV because so many of my women clients had been to five or fifteen doctors and not been diagnosed.

The symptoms of VV are severe pain with pressure (biking, tight pants) and burning, stinging, or a raw sensation within the vestibular area (opening to the vagina). In acute VV, the woman can't endure sitting in a chair and can't wear underpants. Obviously, intercourse is out of the question.

An estimated quarter million women in the United States alone suffer from vestibulitis, which is a real medical condition, not psychological avoidance. For years, physicians dismissed it as psychosomatic, until someone thought to examine the tissues under a microscope. Sure enough, there were pain cells a-plenty. Because VV is so frequently undiagnosed, male partners often don't understand how painful it can be for a woman. Even the touch of a Q-tip can feel like a sharp instrument—hence the name "Q-tip test" that doctors use in diagnosing it.

I have found many ways to help a VV patient, in addition to the treatment from her physician:

- Identifying and reducing stressors in her life
- Teaching her the relaxation response, including imagery to ease symptoms
- Using relationship and communication coaching

Finally, it's important for couples dealing with VV to relearn how to be sensual and sexual in many ways, not just intercourse, and to be open to other techniques and positions when intercourse can be resumed.

Less Common Causes of Painful Intercourse
Painful intercourse can also be caused or worsened by a low-grade yeast infection, a chronic inflammation of the bladder called interstitial cystisis, fibromyalgia, endometriosis, and a hormone imbalance. A physician should rule out all of these possible causes before the woman either does nothing and simply tolerates infrequent sex, or refrains from sexual activity altogether.

Some Other Sexual Dysfunctions

These are some common performance problems you likely know about but may not fully understand why they happen, or how to deal with them.

Orgasm Difficulty

The inability to climax easily, or at all, is also called anorgasmia. In past years, this was the most common problem presented by my clients. Nowadays it is less so, but it's still a frustration for many.

In men, it falls under the category of delayed ejaculation (keep reading for an explanation). Mostly, though, it is a problem for women. The first challenge is expectations. Our media, fiction writers, porn producers, and other fantasists would have you believe that good hard sex always culminates in a shrieking orgasm for the woman.

Not true. A majority of women do not reach orgasm through penile thrusting. Most women need clitoral stimulation as well, from either themselves or their partner. Some women simply reach down between their two bodies and use a hand manipulation to excite the clitoris, or their partner does that. Others like to bring a vibrator into play, buzzing both pelvises.

Some women greatly enjoy the delight, sensuality, and closeness of intercourse but are shy about their climax. These women prefer to bring themselves to climax in private. Their beloveds might feel a little left out but still love their together-sex.

Premature Ejaculation

Gentlemen, learn the squeeze technique. Here's how it goes: as you masturbate, when you get close to coming but before you've reached the point of no return, stop stroking and tightly squeeze the glans of your penis (the bottom of the fireman's helmet, if you're circumcised). Put your thumb on one side and middle three fingers on the other, and really squeeze tightly. When the urge to ejaculate has passed (and your penis may wilt a little, too), start stroking again, and then repeat the process.

When you've mastered it, on another occasion, squeeze the base of your penis instead of the head. This, too, will slow you down. When you are making love to your lady and feel ejaculation heading your way, you can pull out of her slightly till you can reach the base of your penis, and squeeze, or have her squeeze, to slow you down. This can actually be fun, and most partners are happy to help. You are actually creating new neural pathways in your brain, new patterns of arousal and control.

Another technique is called stop-and-start. When you're close, just stop moving till the urge passes.

Delayed Ejaculation

This occurs when the man takes longer to come than he or his partner wants. It's not very common, which is a good thing, because it's also hard to treat. However, it can cease to be a barrier to pleasure if the couple simply communicates. If the woman has had about all she can enjoy, she can say, "Honey, I love to rock-and-roll with you, but I'm wearing out a bit." And he can either finish himself off by hand or she can help with her hand and mouth. Whatever fits for each couple.

The best way for a man to overcome delayed ejaculation is to (drum roll, here it comes again) pay attention to the pleasurable sensations and turn off the "thinkety-think" mind chatter. Don't worry, don't obsess, don't try hard—just relax and go with your body.

Cultural and Religious Issues Affecting Sex

In the past several years, I have had a surprising influx of couples, some from other cultures, who have been married two or three years but have never consummated their marriage. Though the backgrounds differ, their stories are similar. They were both virgins, usually because of cultural custom or religious prohibition against sex before marriage. If they were from another culture, perhaps they had spent very little time alone. Other couples had had every kind of sex play together, totally naked, but were saving intercourse for marriage.

Here the stories merge. On their wedding night, the new husband, perhaps uneducated in ways to arouse a woman, tried to penetrate his virginal wife, who shrieked in pain. They drew back, horrified, and decided to wait a couple of days before trying again. The next time they tried, it was the same story, even with the couples who'd had heavy petting and oral sex.

This cycle continued for years. Every few weeks, they would try again, unsuccessfully. Penetration had become their only goal. After a while, the husband began to have erectile problems. He literally wilted at the thought of hurting her again. Meantime, the wife had settled into a different mindset: either she expected him to do his duty even if it hurt her, because he's the man and is supposed to, or else she withdrew altogether.

This stress is often exacerbated in couples from India, Africa, or the Middle East. Back home, their parents are concerned that they have not yet become pregnant and are pressuring them to start having babies. Of course, the young couple is too embarrassed to tell Mother and Dad what's going on. They also fear that dominant parents will force them to divorce.

Obviously, lubrication is a big issue. How can an inexperienced woman get wet with arousal when all she can anticipate is more pain? In some cases, there is also a significant disparity in size; the woman is so tight that she requires a child speculum to even have a pelvic exam. Talk about a challenge! My best approach with these couples is to teach them relaxation, perhaps with hypnosis, and a lot of badly needed education. Many of them eventually do get sexually active, but some just don't come back after a session or two.

My favorite memory of this situation, a happy one, is about a couple from Europe who moved to the States. While still back home, they discovered that she had vaginismus and went into such vaginal spasms that only a finger could get into her vagina. Their doctor said, "Don't worry. As soon as you have a child, your body will realize that the birth canal can accommodate a seven-pound baby, and your husband's penis will no longer be intimidating." Well, yeah … but how were they going to get pregnant?

Easy, said the old-fashioned doctor. He instructed the husband to put a steel mixing bowl through the dishwasher cycle to sanitize it, and then to ejaculate into the bowl. They would then use a syringe to extract the semen and insert it into her vagina at a time when she was fertile. It worked the first time they tried. She had a perfect pregnancy, and then at the last minute during her labor, there was a problem and she had to have a C-section.

But here's the most interesting part. They came from a progressive society and had an absolutely marvelous sex life. Almost every night they made out, caressed, stroked, licked, kissed, sucked, brought each other to orgasm, and became ever more connected. When they came to see me for help to finally be able to have intercourse, they were glowing with love. They just wanted to be "normal." We ascertained that she was one of the few women with vaginismus who'd had a happy and safe upbringing with no sexual abuse or accidents. There was just no accounting for her condition.

For weeks we had therapy sessions and they worked on homework assignments, but they looked more haggard each time I saw them. After a while I said, "Kids, I have clients who would literally give a million dollars to get the exuberant, joyous sex life you have. Why not just accept that this is the way you two make love?" They were clearly relieved and left therapy with my blessing.

A few months later, the gynecologist who'd referred them in the first place called me and said, "Well, you are a miracle worker. They're pregnant!" And I answered, "Much as I'd like to take part of the credit, you might ask them if a steel bowl was involved." I hear that they now have three children, all born C-section. I hope they're still one of the sexiest couples on earth.

The Problem with Cybersex

Before I close this section on roadblocks to *Sizzling Sex,* I want to say a word about cybersex, which might be likened to a fantasy that can mushroom into Godzilla and crush healthy sexuality. It's true that a little porn shared by consenting adults can provide a great jump-start to a sexy evening, just as a glass of wine with dinner can enhance the meal. But while a glass or two of wine is fine for most people, some people cannot stop after the second, or the third, or the eighth glass. They have become addicted to alcohol, and it can ruin their lives and destroy their families.

The same is true of online porn, an extremely addictive "substance" and a growing problem for many men. It's free, it's accessible 24/7, it's there late at night when everyone else is asleep, and it gives a fast high and payoff. It can get out of control so fast, it's like a sped-up movie. It can lead the cybersex user to indulge in online chats with an alleged beauty (probably a hairy guy with a cigar in his mouth), to loss of anonymity, and finally to catastrophic career- and marriage-threatening discovery.

I don't know how many men are addicted to Internet sex; there may not be an official statistic yet. But it doesn't much matter. I, along with most other marriage and sex therapists, can see it's a problem that's growing almost exponentially. In my own practice, at least once a month I have a new client couple whose relationship has been blown apart by the husband's addiction to online porn. So enjoy yourself, but be smart. Don't get hooked on the crack cocaine of fantasies. If the addiction begins to negatively impact your relationship and/or other areas of your life, it's time for the addict to consult an individual psychotherapist.

To Sum Up

Men with a sexual dysfunction should have themselves checked out by a physician to be sure there's no hormonal imbalance, chemical reaction, or organic problems such as vascular blockage, high blood pressure, prolonged heavy smoking, or alcoholism.

Women should see a gynecologist to rule out hormonal imbalance (including low testosterone), structural abnormalities, yeast infection, or chronic conditions such as vestibulitis.

Dysfunction has four general causes: physical, chemical, psychological, and interpersonal (relationship). If your physician finds no organic or chemical reason for your dysfunction, and if the approaches I've offered here don't work, it's time to find an AASECT-certified (American Association of Sex Educators, Counselors, and Therapists) sex therapist in your area.

Go to www.aasect.org and, on the left side of its home page, under "Locate a Professional," click on your country and then your state. You'll receive a list from which to choose. For example, in my state, Texas, there are three AASECT-certified sex therapists in my Dallas area.

To enjoy the natural flow of your sexuality, you need to identify and release the logjams that impede that flow. Your sex therapist can help with any psychological or relational causes of your problem, working respectfully with you and your partner, and can also help you to reprogram your physical responses through sensuality exercises at home.

Don't put up with frustration and loss of intimacy. You deserve more!

A SPICE CALLED VARIETY

I can think of no better advice for long-lasting *Sizzling Sex* than "Keep it new." By this, I don't mean you should exhaust yourselves in a never-ending search for novelty, whether through new positions or sex toys, any more than you would search out new partners. Plenty of resources out there can guide you to adventurous positions for sexual intercourse that you may wish to introduce into your sex play; *The Complete Idiot's Guide to Amazing Sex, Third Edition,* is one good one to start with; I list others in my bibliography.

But newness is, first and foremost, a state of mind: a curiosity about your partner and your sexuality that encompasses everything you don't yet know about your partner (beginning with the premise that there's plenty you don't know!). Next, you must maintain a health curiosity about all the ways you have not yet found to explore each other and your sexuality. Of course, it all begins with a solid relationship.

I'm often asked what it takes to create a relationship that lasts. Here's my list of absolutes, as in "absolutely must do" to keep a relationship fresh and growing. Not all of this advice gets *acted out* in the bedroom. But, I assure you, if you follow these guidelines for a good relationship, good results will absolutely *show up* in the bedroom.

- *Commitment.* This could be called the "We'll work it out, babe" attitude. It's about being willing to put energy and understanding into the relationship, not being poised for flight.

- *Minimum of drama.* Be willing to use your good sense, your rational brain, and your emotions. Avoid struggle, effort, martyrdom, blame, and shame.

- *Affection.* Being in a committed relationship means showing those loving behaviors that your beloved experiences as caring. These may include touching, kissing, cuddling, helping with work, using love words, and showing loyalty.

- *Appreciation.* This includes compliments, validation, acknowledgment, and admiration, and not taking for granted the considerable contribution each of you makes.

- *Attention.* This means putting aside distractions when the other person is asking to talk, or finding a time when you both can be really present. Talk *with,* not *at,* each other.

- *Responsibility.* It's about keeping your word, doing your share, working as a team. It's owning your part of a problem and not scapegoating the other guy.

- *Taking care of yourself.* The healthy partner has an identity besides being a mate, knows how to ask directly for what he wants, and meets her own needs without expecting the beloved to be a rescuer.

- *Pleasure.* Successful couples know how to enjoy each other. They basically *like* each other and show it. They find ways to enjoy life and each other.

- *Change.* All successful couples manage to create ways and times for renewal and growth. The partners actively encourage each other to stretch.

- *Flexible roles.* Sometimes he's a good daddy to her, sometimes she's a nurturing mother to him, and they both get to be kids. Different times call for different roles. You get to take turns.

- *Sexiness and sensuality.* Yes, it's about putting romance and love back in lovemaking. Enjoy the look, sound, scent, feel, and taste of your partner.

As you look back over this list, notice how relevant they are to single people as well as couples. You don't have to be in a committed relationship to enjoy, respect, and care for yourself. You can be your own best friend. As a special dividend, you will attract others like you, both men and women, to be your friends. Perhaps one will morph into your beloved. That's what happened to me. I heartily recommend being best friends first, then lovers, to build a solid and authentic foundation.

Appendix A

SIZZLING SEX TUNE-UP

Periodically, it's a good idea to step back and see how you're faring both in and out of bed. Here are some handy checkpoints to help keep your life—especially your sex life—humming:

- Have you managed to slow down to enjoy your life every day? Go back to the basics, beginning with your five senses: take deep breaths, relax, feel your body and the immediate environment. More about *awakening your senses* in Chapter 4.

- Are the two of you having *loving talks?* If not, return to Chapter 5 for a review.

- Has your sex life gone back to being a series of quick snacks instead of a feast? It's time to rediscover the *joys of kisses and caresses* in Chapter 5.

- Have you settled into too much of a bedroom routine? How about revisiting some playful fantasies? Check out the possibilities of *fun and games* in Chapter 7.

- If you're feeling out of sorts with your own body, I have two tips: the joys of self-pleasuring (see Chapter 8) and a day of self-pampering (see Chapter 5).

- Romance yourself. Splurge on silk pajamas or fancy lingerie. Soak in a bubble bath by candlelight and music. Do whatever will make you feel great.

- Rekindle a friendship. When you really pay attention and look around, you'll find you have lots of playmates in your life. Give some ingenious loving attention to them. Make a monthly date to have lunch or an after-work drink with an old buddy. Or use the phone to catch up with a friend who's far away.

- Get experimental. Never eaten Ethiopian or Vietnamese or Russian food? Give it a try. Take a class in ethnic cooking, or invite some friends to visit an unfamiliar restaurant. Find a sidewalk fair or an art show. Take the train to a nearby town and walk around. Start a conversation with the person behind you in line at the movies. Take swing or line dancing or tango lessons. Why not? You'll meet other adventurous souls there, and you might actually get good at dancing.

- Connect with the passion for life. Take yourself seriously but not solemnly or in a self-centered kind of way. Become loving, tender, and playful with yourself and others. In other words, celebrate the amazing gift of life, sensuality, and joyous pleasure.

Appendix B

RESOURCES FOR *SIZZLING SEX IN 30 DAYS*

There are many useful books and websites available offering more tasteful and educational information in every area we've covered. Just a note of caution: because sexuality as a topic or a search parameter can bring the vulgar along with the informative, you may have to look past the former to get to the latter. This tends to be more of an issue when surfing on the wild and wooly Internet, and less so when ordering specific book titles. Each of the books recommended below is one I highly recommend.

RECOMMENDED BOOKS

Here are some of my favorite books to help your *Sizzling Sex* and the relationship that goes with your newly rekindled intimacy.

Barbach, Lonnie Garfield. *For Each Other: Sharing Sexual Intimacy.* Seattle: Signet Press, 2001.

Berman, Jennifer, and Laura Berman. *For Women Only.* New York: Holt, 2005.

Cassell, Carol. *Put Passion First.* New York: McGraw Hill, 2007.

Faber, Adele, and Mazlish, Elaine. *How To Talk So Kids Will Listen and Listen So Kids Will Talk.* New York: Collins, 1999. (Not just for kids!)

Hendrix, Harville. *Getting the Love You Want: A Guide for Couples.* New York: Holt, 2001.

Hutcherson, Hilda. *Pleasure: A Woman's Guide to Getting the Sex You Want, Need, and Deserve.* New York: Putnam, 2003.

Kaplan, Helen Singer. *How to Overcome Premature Ejaculation.* Florence, KY: Brunner/Mazel, 1989.

Locker, Sari. *The Complete Idiot's Guide to Amazing Sex.* New York: Alpha, 2005.

Love, Patricia, Dr. *Hot Monogamy: Essential Steps to More Passionate, Intimate Lovemaking.* New York: Plume, 1995.

Van Meter, Roz. *Put Your Big Girl Panties On and Deal with It.* Naperville, IL: Sourcebooks, Inc., 2007.

Zilbergeld, Bernie. *The New Male Sexuality, Revised Edition.* New York: Bantam, 1999.

Zoldbrod, Aline. *Sex Smart.* Berkeley: New Harbinger, 1998.

RECOMMENDED WEBSITES

For sex education, toys, and other adult products, check out these websites. Please know that these sites include a full range of sexual products, many of which may be a bit raunchy. As always, just choose what is right for you. All of these vendors should offer discreet mailing for any products purchased.

- **Good Vibrations**—Sex education, community, and products: www.goodvibes.com
- **Bettersex**—Good source of excellent DVDs: www.bettersex.com
- **Eve's Garden**—Sex toys and testimonials: www.evesgarden.com
- **MyPleasure.com**—Female-centered sex toys: www.mypleasure. com
- **Adam and Eve**—Adult DVDs, toys for males and females: www. adameve.com
- **Too Timid**—Starter sex toys and articles: www.tootimid.com
- **The Marriage Bed**—Sex education with a Christian slant: www. themarriagebed.com
- **www.Roz Van Meter.com**— Section on Relationship Smarts
- **Sexuality Coach**—General information about sex and relationships: www.sexualitycoach.com